LESBIANS TALK VIOLENT RELATIONSHIPS

Affirmations

You are not the only one
Abusive relationships happen to women of all ages, classes, races, dis/abilities, religions, with or without children

You are not to blame
You are not responsible for the abuse. Your abuser has choices of other ways to react

You cannot change your abuser's behaviour
You will have already noticed that it does not make any difference what you do to pacify her, she will continue to be violent or threatening. The only way for the abuser to change is for her to realise she has a problem and to seek help

Ignoring violent abuse is dangerous
Violent abuse rarely happens only once. It will usually get worse the longer it continues. Many abusive women appear to go to pieces after an assault or if their lovers threaten to leave them, and are full of apologies and promises. Unfortunately, experience shows that the remorse will be short-lived and the violence will return

Break the silence; don't remain isolated
You have nothing to be ashamed of. Don't keep the abuse a secret. Get support from someone you trust or contact one of the organisations listed at the end of this book. The more isolated you are, the harder it becomes to take action. There are many people who can and will help you. Don't suffer alone

There is life after an abusive relationship
Though it may seem difficult to take the advice offered in this book, there are benefits. Many of us start new and rewarding lives and discover the exhilaration of being self-sufficient and growing women again. All of us speak of the joy of discovering that the things our abusers told us (you're stupid/ugly/useless/no one else will have you/you'll never make it on your own) were lies

Adapted from London Borough of Camden's 'Domestic Violence' information and advice pack

LESBIANS TALK

Violent relationships

Joelle Taylor
and Tracey Chandler

Scarlet Press

Acknowledgements

We would like to thank Vicky Wilson and Belinda Budge for believing in this book even when we found it too painful to do so. None of this would have been possible without your support and patience. A debt of great personal gratitude is also due to the women of the Child and Woman Abuse Studies Unit at the University of North London for their collective advice, inspiration, and just for being there. Thank you. We would also like to thank the many women who felt unable to contribute to this book, but whose stories validated our own experiences and reinforced our sense of the desperate need for its publication. But most of all we thank the strong and compassionate women who contributed their sentences, their voices and their anger. This book is dedicated to you, and to all survivors.

Joelle I would like to thank Tee for always being the first to arrive and the last to leave – you are a divine and determined inspiration. Thanks to Loulabelle for her perfect posture and perfect friendship, Mel Steel for doing my homework, Vanessa Lee and Spin/Stir for never giving up, and the Fictional Girlfriend for her very real personality. I would also like to tug my forelock to Rose, Bee, Alison, Jed, Kat, Des, Flossy, Dixie, Ruth and Jo for their survival, insolence, strength and courage in the face of techno. Bless.

Tracey First, big thanks to Joelle for her bravery and strength, thanks to Mandy Head, Annie and Jessie, and Yvonne Siddiqui – women who drew the pieces together again into a whole woman. Treasured gratitude for Jessie Helen's presence in my spirit. Thanks to the Divas, sisters in all things progressive: Lesley, Colleen and Anna. Finally, thank you to my mother Helen for her love and example in being true to yourself. And to the many other women in my life who show me the beauty that exists in spite of it all.

Published by Scarlet Press, 5 Montague Road, London E8 2HN

Copyright © Joelle Taylor and Tracey Chandler 1995

British Library Cataloguing-in-Publication Data
A catalogue record for this book is available from the British Library
ISBN 1 85727 032 0

Series editors: Belinda Budge and Vicky Wilson
Cover design: Pat Kahn
Typesetting: Kathryn Holliday
Printed in Great Britain

Contents

Contributors

Julie Bindel is a founder member of Justice for Women

Pat Califia is a San Francisco-based writer and campaigner for S/M rights and awareness

Jean Cross is a worker at West Hampstead Women's Centre

Liz Kelly works in the Child and Woman Abuse Studies Unit, University of North London

Joan Nestle is a founder member of the New York Lesbian Herstory Archives and a writer and campaigner on butch-femme and other issues

Femi Otitoju is an equal opportunities trainer and consultant

Bernie Parks is a former WAFE (Womens Aid Federation of England) worker and MA student researching abusive lesbian relationships

Jill Radford is a legal advisor with Rights of Women

Linda Regan works at the Child and Woman Abuse Studies Unit, University of North London

Vicky Watson is a refuge worker for Women's Aid Ltd

This book also contains stories from sixteen survivors. In order to protect their anonymity we are unable to print monitoring details

Joelle Taylor is joint artistic director of Spin/Stir women's physical theatre collective. Her performance piece *Naming*, about father-daughter rape, was premiered at the Oval House theatre in 1994, and she is currently working on her second play, *Whorror Stories*. She has published poetry and prose in a number of magazines and contributed to *Holding Out*, an anthology of short stories by women (Commonword Press). She has been writing and acting on the issue of abusive lesbian relationships with Tracey Chandler since 1992.

Tracey Helen Chandler currently works in the voluntary sector for homeless people. She has published poems and prose in anthologies and publications, and contributed research into abusive lesbian relationships to the Open Space programme *Unspeakable Acts*. She identifies as a power-femme, and is enjoying a renaissance in her creativity and all things camp. She is one of a team of Divas currently scouting London for a venue to promote the diverse talents of women-loving-women.

Preface

We are both survivors of abusive lesbian relationships. It has taken two years and two months to form these words, and even longer to believe them.

We were always sorry. Sorry when we were kicked. Sorry when we were controlled. Sorry for not saying the right thing – at the right time – with the right smile – in the right clothes. Apologising for her punches.

We are not sorry any more. We are not sorry for being abused by the women we loved. We are not sorry for bringing abuse to the attention of our community. And we are not sorry for attempting to stimulate debate. We are not even sorry for not being sorry.

We have always understood that we would be placing ourselves in a vulnerable position by publishing this book. These are our real names, we are real women who can really be found by our former lovers. Our greatest fear, though, is of our community's response. Some will label us 'attention seekers' (as though our personalities were the issue), or simply as divisive, as shifting the focus away from male violence. The issue of abusive lesbian relationships has yet to be taken seriously by our communities because it is a challenge to what we all hoped and some of us believed to be a safe lifestyle among women. Our personal experience, and that of other women who have survived and are surviving violence and intimidation from other women, is perceived as confrontational whenever we open our mouths. But we remain solid in our conviction that it is only by dealing with the things that make our communities unsafe that we can grow towards the utopia some of us seek.

Everyone involved in this project has taken risks so that other women need not. We have worked hard to de-sensationalise the issue and to create a political context within which debate can develop. This is the result. A beginning. This book marks the transition from 'victim' to survivor, from silence into speech, and from speech into positive action. It is a resource handbook for those women undergoing or escaping violent relationships and for those working with abused women within the statutory services. Most of all, it is an archive of women's stories, an affirmation to all survivors, and a clear message to all abusers: **we take back all of our apologies.**

We welcome any communication on this issue.

Introduction: contexts

The backlash against feminism

The issue of violent lesbian relationships is of crucial significance, not only to the lesbian communities, but to feminism in general. When a woman punches, the repercussions of her act are felt far beyond the confines of her living room. This book is set against a backdrop of renewed attacks upon feminism and, by extension, upon the rights of all women. The issue of abusive lesbian relationships has been used to undermine arguments fundamental to feminist theory and to our understanding of the complex structures that underlie male power. It has been manipulated by academics, statisticians and the 'men suffer too' lobby to attempt to disprove feminist analyses of male violence as a means of maintaining power and control over women. It has been used as proof that patriarchy, sexual difference and socially inscribed gender inequalities are simply figments of the feminist imagination. It *was* all just a dream, after all... As Liz Kelly of the Child and Woman Abuse Studies Unit at the University of North London writes in her groundbreaking article on women's use of violence, 'Unspeakable Acts':

Our caution and irritation at 'women do it too' statements were justified, since the speaker was seldom concerned about the issues, and usually motivated by a desire to dismiss feminist analysis.

The 1990s, and the 'women do it too' generation, have brought an implicit misogyny which suggests that it is somehow worse to be beaten by another woman than by a man. Attempting to attach a hierarchy of suffering to women's experience of violence is both ignorant and damaging. The imperative of the arguments set forth in books and articles with titles like *Deadlier Than the Male* or 'Physical Assaults by Wives: A Major Social Problem' has never been to support the survivors of female/lesbian violence. It has been to present the issues in favour of male perpetrators of violence. And it has been to suggest that female abusers are somehow *more* responsible for their crime than male abusers are.

It is hardly surprising, therefore, that there has been an unwillingness to engage with the issue of violent lesbian relationships in the lesbian/feminist communities, and a raw anger towards those of us who have attempted to develop a debate. And, admittedly, it is sometimes difficult to determine which of those writing about the subject are genuine in their intentions. Lesbian violence is not only a convenient tool for anti-feminist theorists, but has also been plucked clean by both the minority and mainstream press in their search for the unusual and the sensational. Considered opinion rarely sells newspapers. This is not to suggest that the press has been directly hostile to the voice of the survivor, but that, for the main part, it has dealt with the issue as a human-interest story, focusing on the account of a single survivor and failing to offer a political framework within which the story can be contextualised. The politics of abuse, and abuse culture, are overlooked. Within the mainstream media, the narrative is also often accompanied by a regurgitation of misogynist and homophobic untruths and stereotypes. But this time, it comes disguised as compassion.

The lesbian and gay press too has been guilty in degrees of denial (it wasn't long ago that we had problems even publicising our requests for information to help us research this book), ignorance of the issues involved and superficial and unhelpful coverage. The lesbian and gay press can be forgiven to some extent for its caution in approaching the subject. It has, after all, become part of the backlash against sexual politics, and therefore against the essence of our communities.

But now the issue *has* been raised, it is imperative that lesbians lead the debate. If we do not, someone else will appropriate it as part of a discourse which attempts to justify and excuse male violence. It is crucial that lesbians abused by other lesbians are given the space and support to define their experiences, to name the issues involved and to evolve a critique which points towards a resolution, both practical and political. Kelly concludes:

...avoiding the issue of women's use of violence represents as much of a threat as we previously felt talking about it did. If we fail to develop feminist perspectives we are handing over this issue to the professionals and the media.

Gender difference

When analysing and discussing women's violence, it is not enough simply to adapt models of male violence; the realities of gender difference must always be borne in mind. A lesbian does not magically become a man, except in the most symbolic terms, when she beats or sexually assaults her lover. She is still a lesbian, and she is still a woman. Her violence comes from a different place, and will mean something different, both to the woman who uses that violence and to those she is violent towards. Not less, not more, but different. For instance, when a man abuses a woman, there is a social legitimation of the act that is not afforded the abusive lesbian. As Julie Bindel, co-founder of Justice for Women, explained in interview:

Women are not elevated in status by abusive behaviour. In fact, they are often excluded or lose something because of it. Conversely, men's status is maintained and even increased by the manipulation of violence.

If we ignore the role of gender in abuse, then we ignore the seeds of the story. When women use violence it goes against stereotypes of femininity. When lesbians use violence it goes against stereotypes of female sexuality. Femi Otitoju elaborates:

Lesbian sexuality is still seen as this cutesy, strokey, supportive kind of thing. Women are seen as being on the receiving end of violence. Men do the beating. The idea that some lesbians can be violent too just doesn't compute with people.

Although our starting point has to be the work already undertaken in studying heterosexual domestic violence, uncritical comparisons to the heterosexual experience are misleading and serve only to mystify the issue further. For instance, women in heterosexual relationships are more likely to be economically trapped than dyke survivors, while fewer lesbian couples have children to provide a further reason to stay together. Bindel continues:

Woman gain no privilege outside that relationship from being violent. In general they don't go along to the pub and brag about it afterwards. They are not advised to 'slap her one' if she gets out of hand. And lesbians are not trapped in the same way that women are with men. Even if you take an extreme situation where two women might have a child or own a house together, they are not bombarded with messages from everywhere else that they mustn't leave that relationship. Usually, their families and communities haven't given their blessing to that relationship in the first place.

This also means that the lesbian has fewer places where her relationship is recognised and which she can approach for support. The emotional impact of domestic violence on a lesbian may well be different, but it is at least as serious.

Research methods

To our knowledge, this is the first book on abusive lesbian relationships to be published in Britain. We did not write it with the intention that it should be seen as the definitive document on the issue, but as an initial overview that we hope will stimulate debate.

When we began to discuss the research methods we would use, we found that our early aim of estimating the extent of the problem was over-ambitious. We possess neither the resources to conduct an accurate national survey, nor the skills needed to interpret the statistics. Given that there has not even been a prevalence survey on the occurrence of heterosexual domestic violence, largely because of the enormous cost of financing such an operation, it became apparent that we would have little chance of securing funding for a systematic survey among lesbians.

Instead, we printed 5,000 leaflets announcing the start of our research for the book and inviting women to submit their stories to us or to contact us to be interviewed. These leaflets were posted to every women's and lesbian organisation we knew of throughout England, Scotland and Wales. They were sent to switchboards, support groups, university/polytechnic women's groups, legal agencies and specific needs groups – for instance, women and alcohol projects. In addition, we advertised in the lesbian and gay, feminist and quality press – attempting to secure the mythical fair representation of lesbians across Britain. Although we believe we have elicited responses from a reasonable sample of lesbians with diverse lifestyles, backgrounds and social experiences, we have inevitably been bound by the women who chose to reply and who had the courage to see this research through to its publication. The women who unravelled their stories before us are from all classes, they are both black and white, they are able bodied and physically challenged, they are new on the scene and they are sick of the scene, they are young and they are old. Some define themselves as sado-masochistic or butch-femme; all define themselves as seeking equality and justice. In order to protect the anonymity and, in some cases, the personal safety of the contributors, we have given each a randomly chosen pseudonym.

While we do not claim that the women included in this book are representative of all sections of the community, they are each of them pioneers, and should be respected as such. They have spoken sentences that they never wanted in their mouths. They have articulated the truths about their lives even though doing so has branded them as liars. They have survived when perhaps all they really wanted to do was to live.

Read these stories with respect. They are a gift.

Naming the abuse

Definitions: speech marks

Developing a vocabulary that defines and describes the experience of abuse at the hands of another woman is an integral part of our recovery process. It is also fundamental to our political and personal understanding of abusive lesbian relationships. Survivors of child sexual abuse and heterosexual domestic violence have long recognised the need to place the words gently back into their own mouths, to evolve a language which allows them to name the violations against themselves as unacceptable and unsolicited. Naming gives speech marks to the silent, allows for a reclamation of the self, is the process of wresting back control of our lives and futures from others. It is for the survivor of an abusive lesbian relationship, not the self-proclaimed experts, professionals or the media, to define her experience, the effects of that experience, the political and personal issues involved, and the ways the community can effectively deal with and work towards resolving the problem. Evolving a vocabulary is pivotal to evolving an accurate analysis.

The majority of work on lesbian domestic violence has been undertaken in the United States, where programmes for both the abused and the abuser have been created. Much of the academic material and articles originated in the US use the term 'battering' to describe the experience. In writing this book, we have found that term restrictive and inadequate to describe the full range of violences – physical, sexual and psychological – that lesbians have faced from other lesbians. It is also a term which has become synonymous with male violence, usually against heterosexual women. For these reasons we use the description 'abusive lesbian relationship', though we recognise that a lesbian does not have to be in a committed relationship with another in order for abuse to take place.

We have chosen the word 'survivor' rather than 'victim' to describe a woman who is on the receiving end of violence in order to emphasise her strength and courage. A survivor may have left her abusive relationship, or she may still be confined within it. But a survivor is not passive. She actively works towards her own protection and recovery. A survivor is not defined by her experience: she defines it. Similarly, we have used the word 'abuser' to represent the violent partner in order to stress the power dynamic at work. The term 'batterer' only describes *what* is being done, not *why* or what is gained by such action. It is a relatively neutral term; it describes without offering a critique.

Abuse is the conscious manipulation of another through the use of threats, coercion, psychological disempowerment, sexual humiliation, and/or force. Abuse is used to elevate one party's sense of personal power at the expense of another's. Abuse is the deliberate disregarding of another's needs and wants in favour of the abuser's own, regardless of the emotional consequences for her partner.

Abuse has a language of its own that the recipient quickly learns in order to survive. She learns how to behave in public, how to behave in private, to whom she may safely speak and to whom she may not. She learns to read between the lines of her lover's face. She learns to be careful.

She learns to restyle her life. She learns to relinquish absolutely her power to her lover. She learns to re-learn.

The abuse is not always focused solely on the partner, but may extend outwards to include the survivor's friends, family and previous or subsequent lovers. This is another method of exerting control over the survivor's actions and attempting to isolate her further from any sense of reality.

Abusive lesbian relationships are democratic in only one sense: they occur irrespective of age, size, physical ability, cultural difference or class status. Although each of these may be a factor in the abuse, they are not causes of the abuse and may not be used as the sole explanation of the origins of that abuse. Possible reasons and causal factors will be discussed in more detail in 'Myths and stereotypes'.

Physical abuse

Physical assaults are the most blatant form of abuse. They are the visible confirmation of a violation that may have been perceived only on an emotional level until this point. Although we have chosen to examine each of the three forms of abuse – physical, sexual and psychological – individually, they are often interdependent: physical assaults will most likely be accompanied by verbal degradation, and the sexual dynamics of violence must not be ignored.

Physical assaults can range from restraint through slapping, punching and kicking to strangulation, stabbing and ultimately death. This is by no means a comprehensive list of the damage inflicted on lesbians by their lovers, but it does give an indication of what we mean by physical abuse. Violence is often used as a mythical 'last resort' by the abuser in her attempts to control her lover's behaviour and personality. It is likely to be preceded by psychological abuse and threats of violence. It is also likely, as we have learned from the patterns of abusive heterosexual relationships, that the violence will escalate, both in terms of its frequency and the seriousness of the injuries inflicted. Long-term physical damage can be caused, and temporary or permanent disability. Whatever the outcome of the use of force, the psychological damage remains long after the superficial wounds have healed.

The body often acts as an archive of abusive experiences. Memories are stored in our skin and bones, and pains from previous assaults may reappear in stressful or similar situations. Glands may rise in the throat following a strangulation and remain swollen for years, or until the psychological conflict within the survivor is resolved. The survivor may be assaulted by an enormous and frightening range of physical symptoms with no discernable medical cause. An arm broken during an attack may begin to cause discomfort again when the survivor is faced with committing herself to a new relationship. The body becomes its own watchdog.

What is clear is that though clinical treatment is imperative after each assault, we must also consider the psychological damage. One bruise can last a lifetime, and cover the entire body.

No woman asks or deserves to be beaten. This is fact. And yet a mythology has developed within the lesbian communities which suggests that abuse which takes place within a lesbian relationship is 'mutual battering': an equal fight, in which one partner happens to be a more effective fighter than the other. The survivor and the abuser are blamed equally. Would the lesbians who conjure up this scenario to explain violence between women place the same interpretation on a heterosexual woman battered by her male partner? Probably not. And here lies the hypocrisy within our communities.

We are all, some of us quite painfully, aware of male violence and we recognise it as the logical outcome of an aggressive masculine socialisation. We are all aware that men are not only trained in coercive strategies, but that they often have the physical mass to carry through their threats, leaving little room for defence and none for attack. There are unlikely to be such extreme physical differences (among the able bodied) between women and there is certainly not the social justification for women who behave violently. So we are able to believe that 'mutual battering' must be the outcome of a problem within a relationship, for which the survivor deserves some share of the blame, rather than a problem created by one partner. As Bernie Parks asks in her paper presented to Womens Aid Federation of England, an affiliation organisation which creates and administers the running policy for the majority of women's refuges in Britain:

Why is it easier to believe an abused lesbian is part of the violence problem, than to believe a heterosexual woman is part of the violence problem?

Once violent behaviour is tolerated, accepted or repeatedly forgiven within a relationship, a pattern of progressive abuse is set in motion. A precedent is announced whereby conflict within the relationship is addressed with violence. The pattern of the abuse often begins with a build-up of tension which is broken by violence. The release of the tension brings a clarity in which the abusive partner recognises the effects of her actions. With recognition come apologies – often genuinely intended – accompanied by feelings of guilt. The feelings of guilt, once the immediate episode has passed, may then be projected on to the abused lover in a classic reworking of the old misogynist excuse, 'she made me do it'. Tension then begins to mount again as the abuser attempts to deny her responsibility for the incident. And the serpent continues to eat its tail. Each time conflict arises, the violence of the assault is likely to increase since there is more to deny, more to feel guilty about, more pressure to release. When physical abuse enters a relationship, it defines it.

Recognising that your relationship is abusive is the first step in resolving the problem. Several women have contributed their personal stories to this book in order to help others to identify their lovers' behaviour as unacceptable and affirm their feelings of being unjustly treated.

A number of motives have been cited as causal factors of violence: feelings of suffocation, jealousy (both sexual and social), and frustration at the abused partner's ability to articulate feelings and thoughts in argument. None of these is an excuse for abusive behaviour. We all experience others' overdependency on us. We do not all resolve this by a physical wrenching away. We all experience jealousy. We do not all inflict pain on our lovers. And we all at times find ourselves choking on our words. For abused women, this is not always a metaphor.

Alison's physical abuse began when she left the home she shared with her lover without explicitly detailing where she was going; her lover suspected her of having an affair with another woman, although this was untrue. She had, in fact, gone to see a close friend to talk about the verbal violence she was experiencing from her partner. When Alison returned home:

She'd phoned the police, my family and everyone in my phone book to find out where I was. When I walked in she started shouting and screaming – she was drunk – then she stood up close and started hitting me. She pulled my jacket over my head and kicked me in the stomach. I didn't hit back, just kept shouting 'Stop!' again and again. It could have lasted two minutes or twenty. She picked me up and let me drip blood on the sofa, gently offering me a cup of tea. She came back from the kitchen and reminded me of her capability of 'pasting me round the walls'. Then she said, 'You want to go, so go.' I fled into the February night with my book bag, my bike, a jacket and a broken nose.

Julia also cites jealousy as her lover's motive:

Three weeks into the relationship I received a call from a previous lover. She rained blows on my head and I fell to the ground. I have had numerous black eyes, broken fingers, broken blood vessels in my nose and horrendous bruising to my body.

Most physical abuse takes place in private. There are occasions, however, when the violence explodes in public, though onlookers may not realise the seriousness of the situation. You can guarantee that any public abuse will be doubled in intensity and ferocity once the couple is alone. Friends and bystanders may also be unaware of the extent of the abused woman's fear when she senses the change in her lover's mood. Kate describes how she attempted to raise awareness of her situation among her friends after violence was threatened outside the home:

It happened in the club. She knocked something out of my hands, then I ran away. I knew that she was going to beat me up, so I ran off. People said that she was looking for me, and that she was crying. That was the first time that I spoke about it. I said, 'You don't know what she's like – don't tell her where I am; I'm hiding.' And I hid around the corner – I could tell by the mood she was in that she was going to hammer me. It was really weird: people kept saying, 'She loves you, she's crying.' But I knew her. Usually, I wouldn't bring it out to the public.

Checklist

The following checklist is a means of helping you to determine whether or not you feel your relationship is abusive. Answering 'yes' to one or more questions is not proof in itself that your lover is an abuser, but it may help you to identify abusive patterns. It is advisable to seek professional help if you are unsure of whether or not you are being abused.

- Are you afraid of your lover?
- Has she ever physically assaulted, or claimed to have assaulted any other woman?
- Have you ever felt sexually violated by her?
- Does she deliberately humiliate you during sex?
- Does she threaten you with physical harm if you do not behave in a way she approves of?
- Does she isolate you from friends/family/ex-lovers?
- Do you attempt to pacify your lover, monitor your behaviour, censor your speech?
- Does she ask/instruct you to do things that you do not want to do/ that are against your moral code?
- Do you feel degraded, insignificant, powerless and/or worthless? Is everything you do dependent on your partner's approval?
- Has your personality, ability to communicate openly, sense of self-confidence, altered to your detriment since the relationship began?
- Does she often overreact to minor events?
- Has she ever physically assaulted you?
- Does she ever restrain your movements – either through physical force or emotional blackmail?
- Does she threaten to injure or kill you if you leave her?
- Does she threaten to expose you as a lesbian to friends, family or colleagues if you leave her?

- Have you ever lied about physical harm inflicted on you by your lover?
- Does loving her make you hate yourself?
- Are you prevented from leaving the relationship by financial dependency or joint ownership of property? Can you discuss this with her?
- Have you ever called the police in order to protect yourself? Have you ever wanted to?
- Are you uncomfortable with allowing your friends to visit your shared home?
- Does she control the relationship/state the terms of the relationship?
- Has she ever threatened or harmed your friends, your pets or your possessions?
- Are you afraid of making your sexual needs known to her?
- Are her sexual/emotional needs the priority in the relationship?
- During an S/M scene are you suddenly unsure of what the rules and boundaries are?
- Are you sometimes/often confused about when a scene begins or ends?
- Does she punish you for what does or doesn't happen in a scene by becoming violent later?
- Are you afraid of expressing sexual attraction to other women/men – not because you may hurt her feelings, but because she may attack you or the person you are attracted to?
- Have you become reliant on drugs or alcohol since entering the relationship? Does your partner control your intake of drugs or alcohol, or actively encourage you to take things which she is aware will harm you?
- Have your eating habits changed to your detriment? Have you lost a considerable amount of weight? Do you find that you eat to console yourself? Does your lover control your diet? Does she continually criticise your physical appearance?
- Does she criticise your intellectual abilities – publicly and/or privately?
- Does she screen your phone calls, and/or read your letters or diaries?

Sexual abuse

Although according to the legal definition, a woman is incapable of raping another woman, we will refer to the sexual violation of a woman by another woman as rape. Rape is not simply a physical act. It has long-term psychological consequences, whether it is committed by a man or a woman. When a woman is the rapist, the only missing element is the penis, and that is easily replaced by a fist, a dildo, or another object. In the context of this book, rape is not defined by whether or not penetration occurred. It is simply the most powerful word available to describe the devastating experience of a woman being forced to have sex against her will. Rape is concerned with the negation of a woman's self, with the denial of her sexual autonomy. As we have learned from research into sexual violence perpetrated by men, it is one of the most effective means of control. It has long been used as a weapon in war, though the emphasis here is on demoralising the male members of the enemy and, by implication, the enemy nation.

Lesbians who are sexually abused by other lesbians often have difficulty in naming the assault as rape. We have no vocabulary for the crime. This was the area of our research that the women who told us their stories found it hardest to speak of. Often they would deny that they had experienced any sexual trauma with their former lovers, only to write later detailing scenes of extensive sexual brutality.

While there is increased recognition of the damaging long-term effects of men's rape of women, the lesbian survivor often has her experience denied, trivialised or dismissed as part of the sexual dynamics of the relationship. It is clear that female sexual coercion is not treated with any seriousness within our communities. Neither the media nor the support services have been prepared to acknowledge its existence, let alone attempt to understand the consequences or provide training that may lead to the provision of appropriate support. We can only recommend that a lesbian attempting to clarify her feelings about a female rape contact a counsellor or therapist who is herself a lesbian and has experience in working with sexual abuse. Even then, she should be careful. Denying the experience is easy to do and – without effective support – often the only option afforded the lesbian survivor.

The physiological consequences of female rape can be as damaging as those of male rape, although there are obvious differences. There is no fear of pregnancy, for instance, and less risk of contracting a sexually transmitted disease. We are not immune, however, from vaginal, cervical and anal infections, which contribute to the survivor's feelings of uncleanliness and of having a permanently tainted body. Violent sex can lead to other physical damage, including kidney problems and pelvic pains. In some cases, a survivor who attempts to suppress her experience may find her body speaking for her when she is under stress. A woman forced to have oral sex, for instance, may develop mouth and throat ulcerations even though there is no direct physical cause. Use of bottles or objects without flanges could create a vacuum in the cervix which could cause permanent damage to internal organs; objects can become lodged within the vagina. Infections such as thrush, candida, gardenia, vaginitis, herpes, chlamydia, hepatitis, intestinal parasites and syphilis can worsen following a violent sexual experience, both because of the stress caused and possible further physical damage. Whatever the extent of the physiological damage, we would advise seeking confidential medical treatment.

The psychological consequences of rape can be even more far reaching. During an act of rape, a woman loses possession of her body. Afterwards she is likely to find it difficult to 'possess' any or all parts of her life again. She will certainly find it problematic to regain her sense of sexual autonomy. She may find herself unable to invest fully in another sexual relationship with a woman. A betrayal of intimate trust is a long time in the healing. This may not be the first time that the survivor has been raped or indecently assaulted by a person she trusted or by a stranger. If this is the case, she may respond to the attack as the final piece of evidence that proves her worthlessness or her complicity in the sexual degradation. She may feel that she has been appropriately treated, that she literally 'got what she deserved'. The sexual histories of both the abused and the abuser are part of the context in which the most recent violation took place, and affect the survivor's ability to understand the experience.

Just as no woman deserves to be beaten, no woman deserves to be sexually humiliated or raped. This includes lesbians who practise sado-masochistic sex. Indeed, there are conscious safety mechanisms incorporated into S/M sex and boundaries and desires are often more openly discussed in these relationships. If you set a boundary within S/M sex and it is ignored or disregarded by your partner, then the sex is not sado-masochistic (a contract): it is abusive.

Different kinds of sexual abuse

Although most of the anecdotal evidence about sexual abuse gathered for this book was concerned with sexual coercion within committed relationships, the experience of 'date rape' or sexual assault from strangers has been noted. Rape of one woman by another can and does occur in all the circumstances in which rape of women by men occurs.

Sexual violations can include deliberate humiliation of one partner by another during sex, being forced to take part in sexual acts one partner is uncomfortable with, S/M sex in a non-consensual context, gang rape, non-consensual scarification of the body and/or genitals, rape with objects, anal rape, and on and on and...

Rape is not rough sex. It is a control tactic. It is power.

Becky suffered continual threats of violence, both physical and sexual:

She continually pressured me to be who she wanted me to be. I had to be a princess and a whore. I had to mother her and be a wife as well. She wanted me to act refined in public but not in bed. I think she enjoyed treating me like I was disgusting. I didn't enjoy that. She'd forced herself on me when I was in bed. I felt she was capable of rape and I was afraid of that too [as well as threats of murder]. She'd continually invaded my physical and sexual space since we'd been finished as lovers, whenever she was alone with me basically. She couldn't seem to see that each time it was a big crisis for me to have someone disregard my right to sexual autonomy, or how much it affected me even though I told her. It felt like constant assault.

Jo felt responsible for being raped, and for the sexual insecurities of the women who raped her:

I went on holiday for a week with a big group of lesbians. During this week I was sexually molested twice, by my lover and another woman I didn't know very well. My lover was being sexual with a number of women and one night she arrived in the communal bedroom where I was alone in the bed in the dark. She got on top of me and tried to make love but I pushed her off. I have to say she was easier to get off than the other woman. I was asleep when she landed on top of me. I came round with her trying to kiss me. I was not as strong as this one and also she took no notice of my protests and my trying to push her off. I probably also wanted to protect her feelings since I didn't want her. I think she was very upset because she felt no one fancied her. She apologised later in a letter but I was always afraid to be alone with this woman after that. The result of these assaults was that I felt it must be something to do with me. I felt I must be giving off victim vibes, or responsible in some way for leading women on without meaning to. The final straw with my lover came when she was abusing me verbally during hitch-hiking. She said she hoped I'd be raped and murdered. Then she added, 'You'd probably enjoy it.' I never trusted her again after that.

Sue had become re-involved with her ex-lover and found that the dynamics between them had changed:

She stopped me from caressing her, took total control of our love-making and hurt me. I figured I'd asked for sex so couldn't complain about what I got.

Rape of lesbians by women known to them is not as uncommon as we would like to believe. Aine describes how her experience affected her:

I think I could call it 'rape' as that's what I'd call it if a man did the same thing. It was from a lesbian I knew slightly who was staying in the house I lived in and who talked me into letting her share my bed. This may sound really naive and stupid of me, but she said she was afraid to sleep alone, and as I'd heard from a mutual friend that she was an incest survivor and had terrible nightmares, I felt sorry for her. I can't cope with describing what actually happened.

It was complicated by the fact that after 'it', memories of incest began to surface for me – first of abuse by my father and then by my mother. This was especially difficult because feminists/lesbians tend to focus on male sexual violence so some women didn't believe me. Also, what I remember my mother doing to me was almost exactly the same as what this other lesbian did. It has been a really difficult three years – for two of them it has been impossible for me to form lesbian/love relationships or be sexual with other women. It would be really good if in your book you could say that sexual and physical violence outside relationships does occur – I've spoken to two other lesbians who have had very similar experiences to mine.

Woman-on-woman rape does not undermine feminist theories of male sexual violence. It reinforces them. Rape is concerned with the self-empowerment of the perpetrator and control of the 'victim'. We have the right to feel as angry and hurt if we are indecently assaulted by a woman as we would if we were assaulted by a man. We have an equal right to feel pain. And we have an equal right to expect care and support from the women's communities.

Psychological abuse

Psychological abuse can precede physical violence and/or run simultaneously with it. Although it is arguably the most common form of abuse, it is rarely treated with a concern in proportion to the damage it causes. It is by its nature a hidden crime: it is difficult to see a damaged sense of self-worth or a shattered identity. Words don't leave bootprints. But they do leave a mark.

Relentless emotional assaults and acts of intimidation can have devastating effects on the abused partner. They create a sense of self-doubt and disbelief in her own instincts or powers to make decisions. Her speech is censored, her behaviour monitored. She learns to read the tread of her lover's feet, to anticipate her anger or annoyance. She is both controlled and negated by her lover's moods. She learns to pacify. She learns to appease. She learns to please.

Psychological abuse is a gentle and gradual process. The possession of another takes time and trust. This creates the central paradox for the abused partner – the indescribable confusion of loving the abuser, of finding a trusted one deliberately attempting to hurt her. It makes little sense: why 'want' someone, why love someone simply in order to hurt her?

The range of abuse is diverse and its progress subtle. It may begin with a casual remark about the clothes she wears and end with her unable to dress herself without complete consultation. It may begin with a public joke about her stupidity and end with her believing she wouldn't have the common sense to survive without her lover.

It would be easier for the abused partner if she could name the act as deliberate, if she could prove some kind of intent. Often, however, it all seems accidental. An attempt at intimidation can easily be disguised by a soft expression and a kiss on the cheek. More often than not, allegations of emotional violence are met with surprised questions about the abused partner's sanity, or at least the reliability of her perceptions. And so she doubts herself and the validity of her feelings even more. Meanwhile, the abusive partner manages to create a perception of herself as the victim in the relationship, the long-suffering Ms Understood.

Methods in her madness

The psychological methods used by abusers to enforce their control are many and varied. An abuser may deny that past violence occurred, or suggest that the survivor was directly responsible – either by her words or her actions. She may accuse the survivor of being the abuser. The abuser may suggest a mutuality in the abuse – a notion that current thinking in the lesbian communities may back up. She may suggest that the survivor is hysterical or irrational, that her judgements are unreliable. She may appear warm and genuinely sensitive to the survivor's needs when she says this. She may seem to be the only woman you can truly trust. Or she may declare that she cannot handle your 'problems' any more, as though they were the focus of the relationship and not the bruise on your left cheek. She may attempt to manipulate you into believing that your behaviour is consciously designed to hurt her, that she has simply been defending herself.

Blaming the victim is a closely followed formula. It involves the projection of guilt from the abuser to the abused. Physical assaults are often followed by justifications which encourage the survivor to feel responsible for the attack, particularly if she has attempted to defend herself physically. Lesbians are more likely to use physical force in their defence than heterosexual women who are under attack, partly because there may be less difference in physical size and partly because of a kind of anti-femininity: we have all had to learn to defend ourselves at some point; we have all at some point rejected the association between femininity and passivity.

Sue found herself being blamed for incidents involving violence if she at any time attempted to defend herself:

She was changing reality there in front of my eyes – she kept saying that she hadn't attacked me once, which was just not true, she did attack me first and she was still constantly going for me. What she did over and over was to take my wrists like in handcuffs and when I fought out of that control she would say that I was attacking her.

Kate was continually verbally and physically abused by her alcoholic lover, who would actively attempt to solicit violence from her so that she would appear to be the partner to blame. And it worked:

It became two-way because I just used to freak. She was screaming at me, being extremely verbally cruel, and I just bit into her lip. Bit her lip off. I just wanted her to shut up.

To suggest that such scenarios are 'mutual battering' is both ludicrous and intensely damaging. It ignores the dynamics of an abusive relationship, the power structures in place and how they affect the survivor. Mutual battering is a myth and an oxymoron. When an abuser attempts to solicit violence from her partner, it is an act of absolution. It releases guilt and reaffirms her notions of the equality of the relationship. It also has the effect of helping to convince the survivor of her own responsibility for the violence, so she becomes an accomplice in her own abuse. This will contribute to the length of time the abused partner is able to remain in the relationship and may become one of the most difficult aspects of the relationship for her to come to terms with. It also encourages silence, so the abuser's secret becomes one that belongs to the relationship.

Isolation from others and confinement to the relationship are common control tactics. When a woman is isolated from her friends and her community, her perception of reality and understanding of acceptable behaviour can be more effectively manipulated by her abuser. She has no point of reference in the 'real world', in a world that may contradict her lover. In this way, the abuser can redefine reality.

All the women interviewed described an enforced separation from their network of friends, their frame of reference. This was achieved in a number of ways. The abuser may assert that the survivor's friends are not 'good' for her, that they are using her, or that they want to destroy the relationship. She may suggest that she feels intimidated or victimised by her lover's friends. Or that all her lover's friends are flirting with her, as happened to Anna:

She would either put my friends down or distort facts to make me distrust them. Or she would say that everyone wanted to sleep with her. Every single person she came into close proximity with. And somehow I believed her.

As time progresses and the abused partner's perception of reality is increasingly distorted, she may begin to recognise these fictitious flaws in her friends herself.

If the abuser is a closeted lesbian, she may request that her lover sever all contact with the lesbian community for the sake of discretion. Sarah describes how her lover tried to control her access to any sense of lesbian identity:

She was so paranoid about anyone knowing about our relationship that I never got involved with the lesbian community, if indeed there is one anywhere near. I bought magazines and books, but that was the only contact I had with the lesbian world.

Lesbian lifestyle is an important ingredient in the construction of lesbian identity. Controlling access to the wider lesbian community is symbolic of the abuser's control of the survivor's access to herself.

On the other hand, the abused partner may be closeted herself and therefore have no communication or contact with other dykes who might help her to name her relationship as abusive. She may choose to isolate herself in order to protect her lover or to protect herself against uncomfortable questions about physical injuries, or the nature of the relationship. She may simply no longer have the confidence to enter a diverse and critical community. She may feel that she cannot have any contact, intimate or otherwise, with other lesbians during or following the abuse.

A lot of my friends were worrying about me but I just cut off from them. I always had a lot of friends and a good social life before. But I just cut off. I didn't want to see the same people and have to say the same things over and over again. I didn't want to change anything – because I loved her too much. And I felt loyal to her. Very loyal. Kate

Persistent degradation and ritual verbal humiliation weaken the abused partner's sense of self-respect and undermine her independence. The constant criticism and ridicule are ways of containing the abused partner, of convincing her that no one else would want her. After all, no one else could possibly bear her behaviour/speech/clothing/cooking/attitude/personality/make-up/hairstyle/laziness/incompetence/stupidity/body – delete as appropriate. There are many examples of the attempted eradication of women in abusive relationships:

She began putting me down over little things: how badly I did things, and insulting me very subtly by implying that I was ugly and old... Deborah

She tried to order me about like a slave – to make her meals, etc. She wanted sex on tap. She hissed at me and called me a bitch in a very vicious way if I didn't do what she wanted. Becky

She would repeatedly tell me that I was ugly, empty-headed and 'common'. She would tear up my underwear and sanitary towels (which she didn't like). She would force me to wear clothes and jewellery I felt uncomfortable in. My relatives were not allowed to visit us. The slightest protest from me would produce a violent action. Julia

Confidence can be further eroded by continual contradiction, to the point where everything the survivor says comes under scrutiny. She may be privately disbelieved or publicly called a liar. Or she may be ignored for days at a time for some small but unmentionable crime. All of this has a profound effect on the survivor's sense of self-worth and contributes to an increasing self-doubt. It also adds to her perception that she is somehow responsible, that she is, in fact, being justly punished.

Gaining unrestricted access to all areas of the abused partner's life is another common control tactic. This can extend to reading personal letters and diaries. In this way, the sanctuary of personal privacy is removed. The survivor may even find herself in a situation where her diet is prescribed by her lover: a control of her capacity to nurture herself that increases dependency and further erases individuality. In a literal possession of her body, the abuser begins to live beneath the survivor's skin. Food intake may also be affected by remarks about her weight and appearance.

The crossing of personal boundaries is an act of oppression, an invasion. The rules of a relationship require a degree of distance between partners that allows for individuality and personal growth. Boundaries permit the development of separate identities and contribute to the evolution of a strong partnership. When personal space is continually trespassed, it leaves the survivor feeling both violated and anxious: she no longer owns even her own thoughts.

Jo describes how information stolen from her diaries was used against her as a control mechanism by her lover:

My lover read all of my diaries from when I was straight. We both thought political conclusions could be drawn from past experiences. She read them while I was away and they turned her on. She kept going on about how submissive I'd been.

Sarah was involved in what she thought was a polygamous relationship. It was not long, however, before she realised her partner's violent possessiveness, which made it necessary for her to cover up a sexual encounter she had had earlier in the relationship. This act of defensive deception fed her feelings of guilt about and responsibility for the abuse:

The lies were a big mistake because she intercepted all my mail and found out things. I felt guilty about lying, and therefore as though I had deserved the results. I ended up feeling suicidal: the only time I have ever weighed up the pros and cons seriously.

The destruction of property belonging to the abused partner is another example of invasion. In Orla's story (see 'Survival stories') she describes how her past, her history and her sense of context were virtually wiped out when her lover burned her personal papers, including letters she had received and pieces she had written over a number of years. It was an obvious attempt at eradicating Orla's sense of self-identity, and effectively named all her words and thoughts as irrelevant and insignificant. Abusive lovers may deliberately choose to destroy possessions that have special meaning for the survivor, either in terms of sentimental value or because they are objects that help her to maintain her feelings of identity and purpose. Anna explains how her symbols of independence, as a writer and a musician, were smashed to pieces by her lover:

She broke my typewriter. And my tape-deck. I was standing outside the room but I just had to let her. There was nothing I could do.

These objects were later replaced by her lover. But what could not be restored was the feeling that her work was respected by the woman she loved and who professed to love her.

Blackmail can be used if the abused lover is closeted, either in her work or among her family or social circle. The abuser may intimidate her lover into remaining in the relationship under threat of disclosing her sexuality if she leaves. A lesbian outed against her will could be subject to harassment from her employers, doubts over her capacity to work with children, or unemployment. Her family may disown her or react in a confrontational manner. She may lose custody of or access to her children. Whatever the circumstances, the power of decision is removed from the survivor. And this is a fear (and often a reality) that lives on long after the relationship has been buried.

Blackmail can work in other ways and be used about any number of revelations. A sexual relationship is the most intimate form of contact and communication between two people. Very few of us censor what we reveal about ourselves and our histories to our lovers. And yet these moments of truth and revelation can also be used to silence and control us. The survivor may, consensually or otherwise, have taken part in acts she no longer feels comfortable with, that she may have moral scruples about, or that individual friends and/or her community would have a problem with. Any number of circumstances can lead to blackmail.

I hated her and was afraid of her. She knew things about me I was ashamed of and I had no doubt that she would use them to keep other lesbians away from me. I felt she had a lot of power over me. Jo

The tyranny of the weak

Often in our research we spoke to women who described their lovers as primarily self-abusive. This could range from alcohol or drug dependency to self-mutilation and threats of/attempts at suicide. These expressions of impotence or anger turned inwards are extremely difficult for survivors to deal with. No one wants to be responsible for another's nervous breakdown or even death. Frequently we understand the roots of the abusive partner's pain, we understand where every punch is born. We can trace the vein of rage in her life, and would do anything to calm and soothe her. When we understand the reasons for her anger, when we recognise her violence as symptomatic of abuses inflicted upon her, then it becomes near impossible to leave her alone with her pain.

The 'experts' would describe this as co-dependency, implying a complicity between the survivor and the abuser. Co-dependency is also known as compassion. As women we have been trained to care for, to nurture and to clean up (both literally and metaphorically) after the people we love. As lesbians we have learned that if we don't care for our lovers, no one else will. Deprived of the extensive support network available to heterosexuals, a lesbian relationship can become a euphemism for 'therapy'. There is limited opportunity for dykes with mental-health problems or serious emotional difficulties to enter into a form of care that deals with their needs, that understands their sexuality and the context of lesbian lifestyle. Relationships can become based on need rather than mutual respect.

The emotional effect of living with a self-abusive lover is profound. The lover controls through her attempts at self-control:

I felt sorry for her at first. She admitted herself to hospital after taking a handful of paracetamol into her mouth, crunching them up and spitting them out. This was about two months after the first time she had hit me. She stayed there for four days and then returned to our flat. I felt guilty, as though it were something I had done to her. And that I deserved the violence; that if I somehow survived it all, maybe she would get better and we could go back to being close. Sarah

Every time I tried to leave her she would hurt herself – she took an overdose, cut her wrists... The emotional blackmail of constant suicide threats and the total control she exercised over my life through her anorexia quite simply meant that I stopped existing as an individual. She diminished me in every way imaginable. I suppose that she ruled through the 'tyranny of the weak'. Even now, after all these years, I find it next to impossible to protect myself from a 'victim'; and she was THE VICTIM par excellence. My way of dealing with this now is: when I spot someone with that victim psychology, I just run for my life. Anna

Psychological consequences

Some of the psychological consequences of living a daily round of fear and degradation have been detailed in the previous chapter. Women spoke of feelings of guilt and responsibility, of an inability to form intimate relationships, and of isolation from friends, family and the lesbian communities. There are few lesbian- specific support services, and even fewer that take account of the differences of racial/cultural origin, sexual practice, class and physical ability that make up our sense of identity. This lack of appropriate support can compound the pain and isolation, naming the survivor as 'other', as different and as separate.

Support

The extent of the impact of the abuse and the length of time it takes the survivor to recover depend in part on the reaction of her immediate support network: her friends, relatives and the wider lesbian communities. If her abusive experience is acknowledged and treated with the seriousness it deserves, it is likely that she will begin to re-build herself sooner and on firmer ground. If the effects of the abuse are denied or trivialised, however, she will find it more problematic to re-establish her trust in her communities, or even in lesbian sexuality. When the survivor's allegations of abuse have been met by her partner with ridicule – as some sort of hysterical hallucination – over a period of time, then it is vital that she receives immediate validation of her experience. She needs to be believed. She needs her experience to be understood on her terms. She does not need to be told that it is she who has the problem. She does not need an embarrassed silence. She does not need enquiries into the sexual nature of her relationship. A lesbian should be able to expect as serious a response to her experience as we demand for women who have suffered violence, sexual or otherwise, from men. Otherwise, she can become emotionally fixed at the moment of abuse. Nancy Hammond, a clinical psychologist working on this issue in the US, elaborates in her paper 'Lesbian Victims of Relationship Violence':

...violence in lesbian relationships does not happen in a vacuum. Friends and family members of both the victim and the batterer play some sort of role in the relationship dynamics, whenever they make choices about whether to

ignore, comment on, or confront abuse. These choices ultimately have an impact on the self-esteem and sense of personal integrity of the concerned person.

Research into child sexual abuse proves how valuable it is to the resurrection of the survivor if she has either a trusted person to whom she can disclose, or a trusted and stable person in the home environment. They serve as reference points. They serve as signposts to something else.

Believing the survivor is lesson number one. Lesson number two is **acting on the information she gives you** – and it *is* a gift to be trusted with such knowledge. Use it well.

Common reactions

Survivors of abusive relationships may suffer **psychological and/or emotional collapse**, either during the abusive period or after the relationship ends. Given the lack of lesbian-specific therapy programmes, it is unsurprising that the problem is sometimes diagnosed as 'lesbianism' itself. The pressures of a violent relationship can give rise to symptoms that range from anxiety and depression through to seizures and self-abusive behaviour. These symptoms are collectively named **post-traumatic stress disorder**, a condition associated with the survival of extreme shock situations such as rape or war, and recognised by the American Psychiatric Association as one of the possible long-term consequences of male violence on women. Hammond describes the characteristics of post-traumatic stress disorder:

...battered lesbians experience nightmares, brief disassociative episodes, and excessive fear in situations that trigger an association to the abuse. Social withdrawal, emotional detachment, hyperalertness or excessive vigilance for danger, concentration problems, sleep disturbance and guilt about the victim's efforts to defend herself are all common.

Post-traumatic stress disorder may often be misdiagnosed as schizophrenia, personality difficulties or even asthma. This serves to reinforce the survivor's belief that she is the source of the problem, and not the relationship or the abusive partner. This is particularly relevant if she has suffered a history of abuse, either with men or women.

Emotional or psychological breakdown can compound and be compounded by the survivor's sense that she really is weak, really is incompetent and unable to care for herself without her abusive partner. Her lover may use the breakdown as evidence against her and suggest that it is the root of all the problems within the relationship. She will often attempt to claim the status of 'victim' herself.

I've had three major depressions, and one lasted three and a half years and that was while I was with her – the whole second half of our

relationship. I felt so low that it was almost 'normal' to feel like shit. She just confirmed my worst fears about myself. She became the personification of my worst nightmares. I just couldn't get out. I have never been so close to suicide in my life. At the end, because she had cut me off from my friends and all my other points of reference, she was the only thing I had. Literally. I felt that if I lost her as well, then I might as well commit suicide. At times, I also felt very strongly that I wanted to kill her. Anna

I felt like a piece of shit. I had a nervous breakdown soon afterwards. I became an alcoholic. My doctor wanted me to have psychiatric treatment but I was frightened I'd be committed and never get out as I was seriously depressed. I didn't tell the doctor what was going on. I was given psychiatric drugs which reacted with the alcohol and caused a physical collapse. I was unable to continue with the course I was on and dropped out. I attacked a man who was behaving in a woman-hating way and apparently just missed killing him. I was arrested and charged with grievous bodily harm. I escaped a prison sentence by pleading guilty to actual bodily harm. Jo

The development of **eating disorders** such as anorexia nervosa or bulimia nervosa is also common – an attempt by the survivor to control herself and her environment through the control of her food intake. In the case of bulimia, the survivor may be subconsciously attempting to build an impenetrable wall between herself and the relentless physical or verbal assaults. This is one more example of the survivor's internalisation of her situation – the literal consumption of her pain. Such disorders are also visible symptoms, a way of wearing our battle scars.

Other women report **uprooting themselves** – either by ostracising themselves from their local community or leaving the area in which they live. Women have given up their claims to homes they have shared with their abusive partners, losing their base, their familiarity, their security. They have been forced to resign from work – either because they have moved away from the area or because the psychological effects of the abuse have made it impossible to continue in full-time employment. Or some may simply need to conceal their bruises and breakages.

I was trying to get out for a long time without her knowing. I was very frightened of her. There was another woman who seemed to be attracted to me. I was terrified [my partner] would notice. In the end I left the area for another job. I finished it, but by then she'd become involved with a woman she'd slept with previously during one of our breaks and didn't pursue me. Becky

I got out by running away to the West Country for two years. I've only recently dared to return to London. Chris

I ended up arriving at work one day, going to the principal's office and

telling her that I was going to have to hand in my notice. Then bursting into tears. She gave me the phone number of a woman who worked in the local Family Centre, who I then went to see. And that was when I realised that I had to get out as soon as possible, before something serious happened to me – at that stage at least four people had warned me that she was capable of killing me, either with her own hands or from illness caused by the emotional upheaval. I did develop glandular fever, and I have had a lump in my neck since then. Sarah

Abused women take responsibility for crimes committed against them. They have learned a pattern of pacifying the abuser: when they cannot prevent violence or evade insult and criticism, they learn to look to themselves. To improve themselves. To become the mythical 'perfect partner'. As we have already written, the abuser will encourage **feelings of guilt and responsibility** in the survivor.

I took responsibility because I allowed her to live in my house. All the warning signs were there. I knew it was the wrong decision, and I still did it. Delilah

I felt 100 per cent responsible. That's why I didn't turn my back on her in the five years after we split up. Everyone kept saying that I had to get on with my own life, but I couldn't turn my back on her. And even though I knew that she was anorexic before she met me, I ended up feeling responsible for that too. And then the suicide threats... Anna

I felt useless, as if the situation was my responsibility. If I was a better person, a different person, the situation would change. I was always trying to meet the demands being made of me, rather than viewing them as unreasonable. Chris

If a survivor has undergone previous abuse, particularly as a child, she may begin to believe that she is subconsciously attracted to abusive people or situations.

My mum is schizophrenic, and I think I'm drawn to women who will punish me like my mum did. I have to have someone to look after. Being intimate with someone as a survivor is really difficult. Kate

I've looked at my values and beliefs and I've realised that I'm not as honest as I thought I was. I put other people first and feel that I have to please them. I attended a personal growth group for a year, and talked a lot about the experience. The facilitator reckoned there was transference from me of my mother on to my lover. But I don't know. I know I went into the relationship in a 'rescuer' position and ended up the 'victim'. Sarah

Co-mothers and the custody of children

Lesbians are depressingly familiar with stories of legal battles with ex-husbands or boyfriends for the custody of children. Sometimes we win, more often we will lose. Our chances of gaining complete custody are increased, however, if we can prove that the father was abusive, towards ourselves or the child, or that he created an unstable home environment – through addiction to substances, perhaps, or negligence.

When two lesbian mothers are involved, the story develops another dimension. Fear of the media and the reaction of the local community – the child's school, for example – will often deter lesbians from seeking a court hearing. Any lesbian who did wish to fight for custody or access to an artificially inseminated child of whom she was not the biological mother would find herself leading a test case. She would be further deterred by the possible homophobia of the court, and the very real fear of the judge ruling that the child be taken into care or even placed with the biological father or family of the biological mother. The legal right of custody would usually remain with the biological mother, though what might happen in cases where couples have been awarded joint custody through the courts prior to the relationship breaking up remains to be seen. Gloria, a co-mother, tells her story:

I wasn't the biological mother of the child we chose to bring into this world, but I was a mother still – in all senses of the word. After she beat me, I knew I had to get out of the relationship. I felt that she had taken me as low as I could get. It took six months to find a decent place to live, during which time she continued to threaten me (somehow, not being her lover any more denied her the right to hit me) and to tell me how useless I was as a mother. I still put 100 per cent into our daughter, because she was my daughter, but my ex-lover relegated me to being the babysitter. When I moved out and she couldn't physically or verbally keep me down, she stopped me from seeing my daughter. It was her ultimate way of hurting me. The pain of that loss was, and still very much is, indescribable. I would rather she beat me to a pulp than go through that again. I fully understand the madness that women go through when they lose a child. It's like she's dead even though she lives just a couple of miles away. Added to that is the myth that if you are the non-biological mother, you are somehow supposed to be able to cut off from your relationship with your child. Bullshit. To love a child is to love a child is to love a child.

Survival stories

In order to help women using this book to recognise or identify with abusive situations, we have printed two complete stories in this chapter. These stories are told in the survivors' own words, and are examples of the courage, determination and compassion common to all the women who helped us in our research. To prevent anonymity being compromised, we cannot give more than the barest monitoring details before each story.

Nadine's story

Nadine is a physically disabled lesbian whose abusive partner was an identified alcoholic.

We went to the same school as each other but were never really friends. Then in 1984 we started having a relationship. It was the first lesbian relationship that either of us had ever had, and for the first couple of months everything was wonderful.

We rented a bigger flat and moved in together. It was only then, when we were actually living together, that I really got to know Claire. We were new to the scene and so were very popular, but along with going to clubs, football, hockey and social occasions went drinking.

I quickly learned that following a drinking session came a beating. It was always put down as my fault for saying, doing or thinking the wrong things. It started gradually with shouting and breaking of furniture, but over the months it progressed to violence which she obviously enjoyed.

It soon became a daily occurrence which I dreaded. The punches and kicks were usually aimed at parts of the body where my bruises would not be readily visible. I did try hitting back a couple of times, but I am not strong and I soon found my beatings were much worse. My only defence was to curl up as small as possible in a ball and pray for it to stop. This would usually be when one of us became unconscious, either Claire would pass out drunk or I would be knocked out.

The next day she was always very sorry. Tears, promises, excuses and the reminder that it was really down to me anyway for annoying her in the first place. The stupid thing is that I fell for it all. I loved her, I pitied her, so how could I blame her? The beatings grew worse and the bruises and cuts were impossible to miss. I sat down and told her that I could take no more. She cried and told me that it was due to her abused childhood and that if I would stay she would make a new start, buy a house with me, give up drinking and get help.

Claire did give up drink for a couple of months and things were much better. She was very touchy and I was still very afraid of her, but she started going to Alcoholics Anonymous and I was hopeful. One of the wives invited me along to Al-Anon. I only went the once, and I saw the raised eyebrows and felt the unfriendly atmosphere because I was open about my lesbianism. I just couldn't cope with prejudice as well at this time. Then Claire had problems at work and used it as an excuse to hit the bottle again.

After fifteen pints of Stella she was worse than ever. She took my car (she couldn't drive) and disappeared for hours. Two friends came around and advised me to lock the doors and not let her in when she returned; they stayed with me for moral support. Eventually she came home and went berserk at being locked out. All the time I could hear her shouting to me to let her in and she would forgive me, but if she had to break in she would have to kill me. Eventually she put her hand through the back door, which was wired glass. I telephoned the police and ambulance and escaped with my friends through the front door.

I spent a few hours at my mother's house before receiving a phone call asking me to go to the station. My mother begged me not to go back to Claire but, as always, I believed it would change. At the police station a smirking PC asked if I would press charges of assault on Claire. When I refused, she was released and we went home together. I spent most of that night in hospital with Claire as she was in such a rage she started to have a major fit.

After that it became less regular and less predictable. She would fly into a fit of rage even when sober and her mental taunting was nearly as bad as her physical attacks. She told me I could never leave her and when on one occasion I listened to the advice of a friend and did not go home despite her demands and threats, she cut her wrists very badly and was taken to hospital, having lost a great deal of blood. I nursed her back to health and through her sobs I promised never to leave again. Then later the suicide threats started and she would take a knife to her throat and then to mine, with the suggestion that she would kill us both and that way we could never be parted by anyone.

I gave up phoning the police because I never had the courage to bring charges against her for fear of what she would do to me later. Social Services were called in by her doctor, who I went to see for help, but who refused to discuss a patient with a non-relative. She was then assigned a psychiatrist, who decided that her main problem was being a lesbian and that she should receive counselling to try to restore her to 'normality'. They didn't even want to know my name, let alone offer me any help in coping or escaping.

To be fair, my mother and close friends all tried to persuade me to leave, but I refused. I still felt a great deal of love for her and wanted to make everything wonderful again. Slowly they all lost patience with me.

Then one of my friends offered me a relationship with her. One thing led to another, and suddenly I felt ready to leave and start anew. Claire took it very calmly at first, although she kept dissolving into floods of tears.

About a week after I moved out to live with Lizzie (that was my new girlfriend), Claire called around to where we were living and said that she was prepared to be friends. I was surprised and delighted. After nearly four years together, and all we had been through, it seemed right to try to call it quits and be friends. That night we all sat in together talking and Claire kept topping up Lizzie's glass.

Claire asked if she could sleep on the settee as it had got so late, and we agreed. I had only been asleep for a short while when I heard a crash downstairs. I ran down to find Claire smashing up the place. As soon as she saw me she started screaming. She told me that she had planned it all and had given Lizzie enough to drink that she wouldn't even hear me.

She had one knee on my throat and the other on my chest when the punches started raining down on me. I closed my eyes and kept seeing the flashes of light which came with every blow. Then she grabbed my hand and started bending back my fingers, ignoring my screams and telling me that it couldn't be hurting that much because I wasn't crying enough. Suddenly I felt relief from pain, Lizzie had awakened to my screams and was now fighting with Claire. This went on for several hours until Claire left, promising to come back. I knew I had only a short time to return to the house we used to share and collect my belongings before she arrived back there herself. I had just filled the car when she arrived and started to smash the car window. I just drove away in terror, not daring even to look at her. After that morning Lizzie and I went away for a two-week foreign holiday and then we stayed for a while with friends in another county.

When we did return we refused to see Claire, although she did turn up on our doorstep occasionally wanting to make trouble. I felt like I would never really be free, just as she had predicted. However, neither Lizzie nor I was prepared for the reaction which we got from our so-called friends on the scene. They totally turned against us, saying poor Claire is so broken since Nadine left her. They said I must have enjoyed the violence which I had received at Claire's hands or I would not have stayed so long with her. It was also implied that I perhaps deserved it, and that there is always a reason for these incidents as they do not just happen in a lesbian relationship as they do between husband and wife. These were supposed to be my friends, and they had been around to see it all, over the years. That hurt almost as much as another beating.

I could not start to explain exactly why I stayed for so long and continued to put up with so much punishment, but I know that at the time my whole feeling was of insecurity and a total lack of self-worth. If you are told something often enough you do come to believe it. I believed that

I could not cope without Claire there, that I was so ugly no one else would ever want me anyway, and that if I dared to leave she would always find me and bring me back or kill me. I was made to leave my job and it was very rare for me to see my family or friends alone. All money was spent on Claire's alcohol and I was not even permitted to choose which clothes to wear each morning.

It was a totally no-win situation. At the time no one wanted to get involved enough to help, and I didn't want to leave Claire. I wanted to make it work. The police thought it was a joke for two women to be fighting, and an inconvenience for them to be called out and involved when I would never press charges. But I was always too scared to press charges as nobody could offer me protection from Claire when she got out. The doctor was a complete blank and the psychiatrist made things worse by insisting the problem was only that Claire was gay. Homophobia was the last thing we needed added to the situation. Along the same lines, it did not help for Al-Anon to take the attitude they did.

No help was really offered to me, but I am not sure if I would have taken it anyway. The hospital repaired two broken wrists, two broken thumbs, a broken ankle, bruised ribs, black eyes and various cuts and bruises, but they never asked how I came to receive these regular injuries.

I would never stay with anyone now who hit me even once. However, I don't know that anyone now in the same situation as I was would have any better alternatives than I did. I never telephoned the London Lesbian Line for help, although I did try to phone the Gay Switchboard on several occasions without success.

I am now in a very happy relationship with another woman. Our relationship is based on love, kindness and friendship. We are just about to celebrate our fourth anniversary. It has not been easy for either of us to come to terms with my past. My present girlfriend has never/would never hit me, but believing that and learning to trust again is a slow process. I still have nightmares about Claire, and even though she doesn't know where I live or my telephone number, I still dread that one day she may find me and call.

Orla's story

Orla is a white working-class dyke of mixed Irish/Jewish parentage. She is thirty-five years old, and lives in Scotland.

When did the abuse start? How long had you been together?
We'd been together for about six months before the abuse started on me, but she was actually abusing herself before then: self-mutilation and I think one attempted suicide. As time progressed, and we were spending more time together, the abuse started.
How did you react to her self-mutilation?
I was upset about it obviously, because you don't want to sit there and see

your lover cut up and distressed about things. I tried to help her, but we didn't seek any professional advice as such. She didn't want professional help, she didn't see her behaviour as a problem – she wanted to work her way through it herself.

How did this progress into her abuse of you?
It set standards within the relationship. She felt that she could abuse herself and from there it moved on so that she could abuse me, could abuse the relationship. She felt it was her right. She was very angry, very upset about a lot of things.

And she felt that she could take it out on others without confronting the problem?
She felt that she *was* confronting it.

What is the first incident that you can remember?
The first incident happened after we'd been out. We'd been drinking and had an argument. It was an attack, very fast and very violent. And out of the blue. The arguments were always quite aggressive, but I didn't feel physically threatened by them. Afterwards, when we analysed it, we kind of thought it was the alcohol and that maybe we should cut drinking. It started off as an equal fight, but it ended with her having me on the ground and kicking me, getting quite out of hand. And there had been quite a lot of blood. On both sides. I managed to kick her, and she was really very shocked about that; shocked about the fact that I'd actually hit back. The next time it happened, it was as a revenge for me hitting her. There was an escalation, and it never went down. It always started from the last point. Which was really difficult, because each time it got more and more violent.

What happened then is that I found I was trying to suppress it; trying to keep her happy, trying to keep her calm. Trying not to have arguments, whereas I found there was no problem with arguing before. But I held my tongue. And I thought about everything I did, being very careful around her.

Did you feel as though you were to blame in some way?
No. I just knew that I was walking on eggshells, and I started to think about whether I could cope with this relationship. I did feel that she needed help, but she didn't want to go to any professionals. As a lesbian, she didn't feel there was any set-up for her. Also, it was very difficult for her to identify herself as an abuser. But she was well aware of what she was doing. She didn't pretend that it was normal behaviour.

Did you identify yourself as being in an abusive relationship at that time?
Yeah. When she expressed that she didn't want professional help, I thought about maybe solving it within the relationship. But I quickly realised that she was too far gone. By then, everything had got out of hand. And she wasn't willing to end the relationship. Which made it very difficult, because it meant that I had to leave my home, and almost go into hiding.

Did you consider alcohol to be a causal factor in the abuse?
We decided that alcohol was something that was aiding it along. It wasn't

the cause. It's stupid to think that drink can turn you into a monster. But we decided that perhaps alcohol didn't help things, and that we should try to be careful.

Did you experience direct psychological abuse?
For about seven months of the relationship, we weren't seeing each other very often. But when she came to London I saw her every day, and that's when it snowballed. Over a short amount of time the worst abuse took place. I experienced her going through my personal stuff; anything I cared for was broken, destroyed, burned. She sat down one day and took all of my writings, my personal photographs, my history, and burned the whole lot.

She was so abusive to herself that at the end I'm quite sure she didn't find it abusive at all. She couldn't understand why I was getting so upset if she could take it. I began to get nervous around her, I became quite frightened of her. I couldn't let it get to a violent point because it always ended up going so far. I was put into hospital twice because of her beatings.

The first time she cracked my ribs, caused me to have a severe asthma attack and also split part of my skull. I stayed in for a day and night to see if I was all right. The second time she stabbed me and I had to have stitches. That was another example of her losing it and getting incredibly violent very quickly. And for no reason as far as I could see – but by then there didn't have to be a reason.

The circumstances were that I'd moved out to somewhere else. At this point the relationship wasn't happening, wasn't on. She turned up and seemed calm so I let her in. It quickly disintegrated into an argument and became very violent and aggressive with things being thrown around the room. There was broken glass everywhere and the room was in a complete state. And she just picked up a piece of glass and stabbed me in the back. Which I wasn't aware of at the time because we were fighting. It wasn't until I saw the blood on the wall that I realised that I'd been stabbed. At that point, I managed to get out. It was really quite frightening; she had threatened to kill me a few times.

And there was another incident. I was running a bath and she came up behind me and plunged my head in the water. And held me down underneath the water. I tried to stay as calm as possible, and held my breath for as long as I could. And at the last minute, she dragged me out. That was the beginning of the incident that led to the first time I was hospitalised. I left and she came out after me, and it progressed into her beating and kicking me. And she used to wear steel-toecapped shoes. I really did feel at one point that she was capable of killing me without even realising it.

Did you ever go to the police?
No. Because I'm a lesbian and she's a lesbian, I wouldn't trust that the sort of help I needed would be given. I was quite prepared to leave the relationship, and sort it out myself. By that stage I wasn't willing to help her. There were actually a couple of times when I threatened to call the police, but I knew that I wouldn't. I don't think they would have been too interested

in trying to solve the problem, they would have been much more interested in other elements: the fact that it was a lesbian relationship.

What was the reaction of the hospital?
The hospitals were quite sympathetic in so far as finding out what had happened, and the second time I told them it was my girlfriend. They just wanted to know whether or not I wanted to press charges, whether I wanted the police involved. They were OK. But the first time I didn't say anything, although they were quite helpful and willing to listen.

How long were you in the relationship, from start to finish?
As a relationship, I suppose seven months. But from start to finish it took about a year. Before I could finally finish it, bury it.

Had you tried to leave before you actually did?
No. Once I decided that there wasn't any help I could give her and that she needed to seek professional advice, I left. And she pursued me.

She raped me as well. Which was the most traumatic. Because of the violence and the feeling that she was out of control, I wasn't very happy having sex with her. And she got really upset about it, she couldn't understand it. She got drunk one night, and that was that. She used her fist.

Did you talk to friends?
At first the response was that they were very concerned for both of us and gave various suggestions. But after a while people just didn't want to hear it. It's not the sort of thing that most lesbians want to hear, especially if you're a recognisable couple. After a week or two, that was the limit: then you should be making decisions.

Did she ever, as far as you are aware, take the violence outside the relationship?
Yes. She would literally just start beating up other people, men as well as women. I think she enjoyed it. She enjoyed the idea of being a strong woman, of people being afraid of her. I think that she was mentally sick.

Was she ever abused herself?
She didn't believe that she'd been sexually abused as a child, but she did feel that she'd been abused in some way. Not physically beaten up, but rejected. She didn't feel like she had a mother, and her father wasn't living. And she just felt that she'd been left to her own devices, left to run wild. Neglect. She was working through it, and she knew she had problems.

How did the abuse progress from the first incident?
What happened next was that she retreated, and the sign was when the self-mutilation would start again. And then the arguments. Then physical fighting, which could take place at any point – it could be in public, it could be in the home.

She was also convinced that I was leaving the house at night, so that would be an excuse for her barricading the doors. She'd wake up in the morning convinced that I'd somehow left the room, gone out and gone off to see someone. And she'd be really nervous if in fact she did wake up and I'd left the room or gone to the toilet. She didn't like that at all. So she started to lock the room up, to try to restrict my movements physically. As much as possible, day and night.

It was an impossible situation. I couldn't live like that. And I was also working, so I had to go out. Most of it was just the pressure of not knowing what was going to happen next, where it was going to come from, and how it was going to be. There would be times when I could walk in and she would literally be in a pool of her own blood, where she'd been cutting herself. But then equally it could be me in a pool of blood.

How did she respond to you having an independent group of friends?
She didn't like that, tried to keep me indoors all to herself. And lots of the time, the self-mutilation would take up so much time and attention that I wasn't seeing my friends anyway. There was a handful of close friends with whom I was able to talk about what was happening, and they would give me advice. They were trying to help – they understood that at that point the relationship did not necessarily have to end. It was only later that it became apparent to everybody, including myself, that this wasn't a relationship: this was a nightmare.

What about your family?
After the stabbing I left the hospital and stayed the night at my mother's house. She didn't know my mother's address. although she had the phone number. My mother was as understanding as she could be; obviously she wasn't happy with me being stabbed.

What did you do the day you decided to leave?
I gave my notice in on the flat, I didn't say anything to her. I packed as much as I could physically carry and left. I'd found a flat somewhere else, and informed a few close friends what I was going to do. And said that whatever happened, they mustn't give her my new address. I had a space of about two months when I didn't see her, when I didn't go out. But unfortunately she must have bumped into someone because she turned up on the doorstep. And it started again. But this time I wouldn't let her in, I used to speak to her through the door. My friends began to get very hostile towards her, and once that happened she backed off. A few times when she turned up, I had people in the flat who spoke to her.

I found that a few women wouldn't believe that it wasn't something I was encouraging. That there wasn't some underlying sexual thing going on between us. That it wasn't basically S/M sex getting out of hand.

Have you/she ever defined yourselves as S/M?
At one point she started talking about it, but I think that was just to confuse the issue.

Almost as a justification for the violence?
A justification as to why violence should be in the relationship somewhere. But it was abusive.

Was she out on the scene?
Yes, she was. It wasn't until after the abuse that I found out that this wasn't her first abusive relationship.

And somehow there had been a silence about this?
A complete silence. Even to the point where I was actually in a room with this woman who had been abused by her, and she never said anything and neither did her friends. I think lesbians are highly protective of each other, we are a small group. They didn't want to point the finger, and they were quite willing to believe that perhaps this time it would be different. Or perhaps the woman blamed herself for it. I don't know. Certainly she was very clever, very manipulative – you could almost feel that it was your fault. But even if it was, no one expects or deserves that response. When I found out about her other relationships, then I realised that was how the violence could escalate so quickly, because she was used to treating women like that. Whereas I'd never come across it on that scale.

You were sexually abused as a child – how did that affect your ability to deal with the abuse?
That was the most shocking: when she raped me. An unbelievable betrayal of trust. I think she was trying to see how far she could go; what would hurt the most.

As a survivor, how do you feel about the 'cycle of abuse' theory, the idea that people who were abused in childhood will become abusers themselves in adulthood?
I've actually found myself wondering how far I can go, how much I can hurt someone when I'm angry. Wishing or wanting to do the same thing. But not. Even in fighting, I found myself stopping myself at a point, and perhaps that's because I see my abuse as completely revolting. I wouldn't wish it on anyone, no matter how far I'm pushed.

Does it make you angry when some women blame their abusive behaviour on their own abused childhoods?
Not angry. Just a bit sad that that's as far as it goes in their heads; that somehow it gives them the right to go out and repeat it. Just because it happened to them. And it's a sad head that's so despairing that this is the only solution it can come up with.

What do you think needs to be done? Do you see this as a political issue?
Completely political. The fact that more women aren't going out chopping other people's heads off because of abuse suffered... the whole range of child abuse, and what it throws up, and the lack of facilities, and the lack of care. The whole structure of society has to change before we can hope to start undoing the amount of abuse that has been done.

How would you tackle the problem?
Talking about it, lots more information. And saying that it is abuse, pointing out that it's not valid. Lots of help, access to refuges. Lesbian-specific facilities. If you tried to go to mainstream facilities, you're faced with people who can't even begin to understand what it means to be a lesbian, let alone tackling the fact that abusive relationships are there.

Myths and stereotypes

Many suggestions have been made about the possible causes of abuse within lesbian relationships. Internalised homophobia, alcohol or drug addictions, violence suffered by the abuser as a child and the power dynamics within a relationship have all been named as possible sources. We have blamed pressure from dominant heterosexual society and culture. We have blamed the glorification of violence within wider society. We have blamed 'abuse culture'. Finally, we have blamed each other.

Not all of the explanations offered have their foundations in fact or unprejudiced thinking. We have searched for scapegoats. Myths and stereotypes have developed – and have even been promoted – to account for abuse within our intimate relationships. These are usually constructed in a way that implies a mutuality or complicity in the abuse; that the structure of the relationship itself is responsible for the violence. More specifically, sado-masochistic and butch-femme relationships are accused not only of causing abuse, but of being where the majority (if not all) of the violence within the lesbian communities takes place.

Before we can begin to untangle the roots of abuse, we need to lay these myths to rest. They serve only to mystify the issue still further, and to prevent us from developing an accurate analysis. Without such an analysis we have no hope of resolving conflict within our communities. We have no hope of providing appropriate support for both the survivor and the abusive partner. We have no hope of change. We have no hope of hope.

Sado-masochism

Sado-masochism has been named as the outlaw sexual practice of the lesbian community. It has been the focus of extensive criticism from lesbian-feminists on the grounds that the introduction of so-called power inequalities into lesbian sexual relationships mimics heterosexual practice and should have no place within the lesbian utopia. In the 1980s S/M dykes faced exclusion from many women's venues and organisations and, by extension, from the debates that helped mould lesbian-feminist analysis. The purpose of this section is not to critique or support S/M, but to argue that abuse is no more prevalent within S/M culture than within other lesbian communities and that sado-masochism does not in itself serve as a source of abusive violence.

It is easy to demonise women who express their sexuality in ways that contradict our utopian visions of lesbian bonding. It is even easier to blame the women involved for lesbian violence, or to suggest that it occurs solely or mainly within their relationships. But **abuse occurs across all sexualities and across all sexual politics.** Even lesbian-feminists can be violent, coercive and controlling... Using sado-masochism as a scapegoat is both unhelpful and dangerous. The implication that abusive relationships occur only as the result of a 'deviant' sexual practice is highly damaging to survivors in non-S/M relationships, who may be discouraged from seeking help, disbelieved or reinforced in their feelings that they or the relationship are responsible for the abuse. It is difficult enough for us to name our experiences as abusive without also having to battle against the idea that abuse happens only on the S/M scene.

Typical of the unproductive outlawing of S/M dykes is the reaction experienced by Jean Cross and Bettina Bell of West Hampstead Women's Centre in the summer of 1993, when they founded a support group for survivors of abusive lesbian relationships and refused to ban S/M lesbians from attending. As Cross explains:

From the beginning we were determined that the group be open to everyone, that our analysis didn't include S/M as violence. Of course, violence can happen in S/M relationships, but then it isn't about S/M: it's about abuse.

This commitment to all sections of the lesbian communities led to bizarre criticisms of the Women's Centre, and even to the suggestion that the group was an S/M stronghold. The point the critics missed is that the policy is about *inclusion*, about providing appropriate support for all dykes who have survived abusive relationships.

One of the most damaging myths about S/M is that the practitioners enjoy abusive violence, and that the masochistic partner derives sexual pleasure from being battered. An S/M dyke no more desires or deserves battery or sexual assault than any other woman. S/M sexual practice is based on consensuality, and consensuality is not abuse. To some extent, S/M is concerned with theatre and the performance of differing power dynamics during sex. Pat Califia, American writer of erotic lesbian fiction (*Macho Sluts* being the most well known) and S/M political activist, writes in her article 'A House Divided: Violence in the Lesbian S/M Community':

Too many women seem to assume that if you are an intense masochist or submissive, there must be something wrong with you. You must be crazy or you must hate yourself. So, if you get hurt, well, what did you expect? This is exactly the same thing as telling a rape victim that she ought not to have gone out after dark wearing a sexy dress.

Yet for some lesbian-feminists, the eroticisation of power dynamics brings lesbian sexuality dangerously close to deplored aspects of heterosexuality, to male violence towards or dominance of women. There is also the fear that performed violence may make other kinds of violence a stronger possibility. Liz Kelly of the Child and Woman Abuse Studies Unit at the University of North London expresses her concern:

Any relationship that is not based on trying to create different models and forms of relationship is more likely to reproduce the patterns that we know are incredibly common in heterosexual relationships.

Meanwhile, S/M dykes *are* being assaulted and abused by their lovers. But the continual attacks on S/M culture have made members of the S/M community reluctant to discuss violence of any kind, or to develop an analysis of abuse. As Califia points out:

There are many good reasons why the violence that some leather dykes commit against each other has remained a dirty secret. We all expend a lot of energy trying to educate the outside world about S/M. We repeatedly have to confront the stereotype that lesbian S/M is the same thing as violence against women. We want to make a distinction between what we do and assault and battery. This can lead to denial that our community, like any besieged minority, has its own problems with the violence.

And because of defensiveness within the S/M community, the perceived antagonism between women's organisations and lesbians who practise S/M, and the direct exclusion of S/M dykes from some support groups, the S/M survivor has nowhere to go. One black S/M dyke equated going to women's organisations for help with going for a cup of tea at the BNP headquarters: the feeling of mistrust is so powerful as to make the very idea appear ridiculous. Almost laughable. Almost. Cross continues:

S/M dykes don't have access to the same kind of venues because they are marginalised by the lesbian community. Politically, I think it's vital to have space for everybody to talk about these issues.

Linda Regan, also of the University of North London Child and Woman Abuse Studies Unit, articulates the opinion of many women working on this issue, who want to see a situation where support can be offered to all women:

I think it is vital that some space is provided for S/M lesbians. It is polarising again. If they have come along to a service they have come because they are in some kind of distress, and I don't think that just because they are into S/M we should then tell them to go somewhere else. I think we have to find a way of responding to it.

Califia concludes her article with advice to S/M dykes on reclaiming denied sections of the women's community:

We must become more involved with grass roots projects that provide services to victims of sexual assault. It is unconscionable that leather dykes are afraid to call rape crisis lines or seek shelter in refuges for battered women. We must demand that representatives of these organisations meet with us and educate themselves about our needs. We shouldn't have to go through therapy to 'cure' our sadomasochism in return for being given sanctuary.

Some form of meeting point is clearly desired by many members of the communities involved with issues of violence and abuse. To equate S/M with violence against women only serves to misrepresent and trivialise the experiences of *all* women who are battered and raped – whether S/M dykes or not. Julie Bindel, co-founder of Justice for Women, speaks of the search to find a bridge between lesbian-feminism and S/M politics:

I think the thing that connects us, more than just being lesbians, is that we are all in some way fighting for liberation, or for an end to an oppression – however we see that oppression. And the only way we can do it is to find some common ground. If black and white women can work together, if radical and socialist feminists can work together, then I think we can work with women involved in S/M. Even if we look at the lowest common denominator. And even if both sides think they are working in a massive contradiction. It's the only way we can start.

Butch and femme

Butch and femme dykes have also had to deal with prejudice from other lesbians and have felt threatened by discussions around abusive lesbian relationships. Joan Nestle, author of *A Restricted Country*, co-founder of the Lesbian Herstory Archives in New York and a self-identified working-class Jewish femme, explains in a letter to the authors:

I pulled back from the early discussion of battering within the lesbian community because I did see it as a coded condemnation of butch-femme passion. I too had known the anger and bullying of lesbian-feminists: some leading lesbian spokeswomen about egalitarian relationships were the most abusive in their private relationships. Yet I have experienced abuse in two relationships; subjects that I have not yet written about, but perhaps I will. In neither case was the woman being the butch the primary cause for the physical abuse. In one case alcoholism was the presenting symptom and in the other, a kind of sexual puritanism that was affronted by my public discussions of sexuality. So I do have much to say from sad experience. I know the complexity of abuse, of the psychological roots, I know the shame and the fear. But I was never willing to discuss this openly in a community that would put an easy tag on my life.

Like S/M dykes, butch-femme lesbians have been seen by lesbian-feminists as simply aping male-female roles, and their relationships have therefore been branded as more likely to include the kind of abusive violence that can accompany heterosexual power inequalities. In addition, there are complaints that the bar scene where butch-femme dykes socialise is one of violence and apoliticism. Given that the bar scene has traditionally been dominated by working-class dykes, and lesbian-feminism in the 1960s and 1970s by white middle-class women, the class prejudice becomes clear. Most of the lesbian role models developed in the 1960s and 1970s derived from middle-class culture and involved a rejection or denial of butch-femme lifestyles as politically unsound. It has taken us a long time to recognise that a violent woman cannot be identified by the clothes she is wearing. But the prejudice has worse ramifications. When we extend the stereotype, we develop the equation butch equals maleness equals violence: the image of the brawling butch beating the passive femme. Researching this book confirmed what we already knew: violence is no more a part of butch-femme relationships than any others, and femmes are as likely to manipulate and brutalise their lovers as butches.

I couldn't tell anyone she was hitting me – me, this Big Butch. No one would have taken me seriously. Sue

Everyone I know who has been socked in the mouth, has been socked in the mouth by the girly... Femi Otitoju

As well as serving to silence the butch who is suffering abuse, stereotyped expectations of butch-femme relationships can give the femme an *expectation* of violence from her lover, so that if she is assaulted, she is more likely to consider it an appropriate part of the relationship. And so she is silenced too.

Race and racism

The racism inherent within society as a whole and within the lesbian community in particular introduces additional complexities when black lesbians are involved in abusive situations, either as abusers or as survivors. It is essential that the experience of black women suffering abuse be listened to and believed. And white women must overcome their fear of being labelled racist and refuse to be silenced if they know that a black woman is an abuser, whether her partner is black or white.

I had a white woman say, 'I didn't want to slag a black woman off to you', and I thought, 'great, leave me to get stabbed in my bed.'
Femi Otitoju

Women of colour continually have to confront stereotypes which name them as sexually dangerous, emotionally unstable and so on. African-Caribbean women are thought to be aggressive; Asian women are seen as automatic victims. Women of colour can therefore be portrayed as natural abusers or as having somehow earned the abuse through their given attitudes and behaviour. It should go without saying that black lesbians are no more likely to use force or coercion than white dykes. And no woman, whatever her race or religion, deserves or asks to be abused.

If white lesbians find it difficult to obtain support from the lesbian communities or from the statutory services, it takes little imagination to envisage the problems black dykes face. Donna describes how difficult she found it to speak out about the physically threatening behaviour of her black ex-partner:

If I'd had more support, I could have gone through with it, but it felt like I was taking the whole community to court

Many black women find the issue deeply painful and a potential threat to communities that provide them with affirmation and support. Because of the racism within the lesbian community, many black dykes feel the need to close ranks and protect their own community from criticism in much the same way as does the lesbian community as a whole. There is a reluctance to 'wash our dirty laundry in public', as one black dyke put it.

As black women we work very hard looking for common ground. Any issue that could divide us, we're often reluctant to address. Femi Otitoju

For black lesbians, it's a problem because we're such a minority and you cannot afford to risk isolation. There's a feeling we should never use the system, always sort things out between ourselves. Donna

There is a silence. When you speak out you lose your community. Now I have no network to support me against the homophobia of the black community as a whole. When you have been through so much and finally thought you'd found where you belong, it's a lot to lose. Sandra

In a racially mixed relationship where the white woman is the abuser, black lesbians we talked to complained that white friends tended to disbelieve their stories or to assume they had in some way provoked the abuse. All of us have a right to feel safe enough to disclose abuse. All of us have a right to have our needs met. All of us have the right to be believed. And all of us have the right to live free from fear. There are stories yet to be told – to be released from the sanctuary of black women's social circles.

I feel I have to be strong about identifying myself as a woman primarily and be aware of and positive about my culture. But also not letting anything that is wrong be ignored, regardless of where it is coming from. I still hope that women in the black lesbian community will see what is happening. They may not have the courage to speak out immediately, but if they can at least acknowledge it within themselves it is a beginning. Donna

Alcohol and drug dependency

She'd have a lager in bed in the morning when I had a cup of tea. Kate

She drank a lot and the shouting would start after that. Alison

Our relationship was very dependent on anti-depressants. You knew about it if she didn't have them. Delilah

Many of the women involved in the creation of this book contributed stories of alcohol or drug misuse, either by their abusive partners or by themselves. Some felt that alcohol was the cause of the violence. Others noted that attacks appeared to coincide with alcohol consumption or follow drug use. Some felt they may well have been beaten anyway. All agreed there was some connection between excessive substance use and the violence meted out to them. It is the nature of that connection that concerns us.

For their paper 'Substance Use as a Correlate of Violence in Intimate Lesbian Relationships', Schilit, Lie and Montagne conducted a seventy-page survey of 104 lesbians in Tuscon in the US. Thirty-nine of those who took part reported past or present abusive relationships. Of that number, 64 per cent declared that alcohol or drugs were involved prior to or during incidents of brutalisation. But rather than draw a distinct cause-and-effect line between the two, the researchers identified substance use as a sign of deeper problems and something that might exacerbate rather than cause violence and abuse:

Alcohol may be used to cope with negative feelings around being lesbian. Because it is in itself a depressant, however, its use only exacerbates problems of self-esteem.

Their findings are backed up by others working with alcohol and drug abuse, who believe that to suggest that alcohol or drug misuse is directly responsible for abusive behaviour is misguided. The drug or the drink are symptoms, not the core problem. The impulse to use violence, and the acceptance of violence as a valid way of dealing with conflict or difficulties, is there before the bottle has been bought.

We know that the batterers' chemical dependence on alcohol or other drugs may intensify their violence but does not cause it. Even when sober and recovering, she remains a batterer. Cuca Hepburn in 'Alive and Well: Lesbian Health Guide', page 171

What drug and alcohol misuse can do is to provide an opportunity for abusive behaviour. Self-control can be considerably diminished, and the feelings of vulnerability or insecurity that sometimes accompany drug or alcohol intake may lead to aggressive actions. Almost as though she were protecting herself from you. The process of addiction to any substance, legal or restricted, is synonymous with tension and depression. In most cases it results in a desperation that, if ignored, may lead to a 'lashing out' or a more considered use of force in order to sustain a habit. Julie Bindel confirms:

I don't believe that alcohol is the cause of it, I think that is a pathetic argument. I do believe that it is a disinhibitor, and that can mean that some women get out of hand.

We are all responsible for our behaviour, no matter what chemicals we have taken into our system, and to blame alcohol or drug use for violent behaviour is to provide excuses for abuse, to make apologies for the abusive partner and to absolve her of moral responsibility for her actions. You cannot buy bruises in bottles. Abusers do not come with labels of proof on the front. Abusers do not come in capsules. They come as our friends.

For Anna's lover, substance addiction was part of a gradually developing pattern of self-abuse. Alcohol and drugs were used to divert attention from deeper difficulties. As Orla's story (see 'Survival stories') shows, having a self-abusive partner compounds rather than diminishes the survivor's pain. And it may well delay her escape from the relationship.

She was a very self-abusive person, and when I met her she was taking lots of drugs. But I was taking drugs too, everyone I knew was taking drugs, so it wasn't an issue as such. About one year into the relationship she started taking smack and getting hooked on it. I asked a friend's advice and she said that I had to tell her 'me or the smack'. Which I did. So she stopped taking the smack but got addicted to alcohol, then stopped the alcohol and became anorexic. Anna

She and her mates seemed to drink a lot. I went along with it and started drinking a lot as well – I thought that was what I should do. Then one night I came home from work and the flat was in chaos. Her nightshirt was wet, and there was something with shit wrapped up in it. I woke her up and asked what had happened. She just verbally abused me. I didn't realise that she was drunk – she had this glazed look in her eyes that was really crazy. This went on for hours and hours. When she woke in the morning she wanted to cuddle me, and I realised that she remembered nothing of the night before. Kate

Some women spoke of being controlled through being forced or encouraged to use drugs or alcohol. The manipulation of substances as a control mechanism has a particularly devastating effect on those survivors who already identify themselves as having problems with addictions. For instance, if the survivor is an alcoholic, the abusive partner may make sure that there is always drink in the home, or constantly suggest opportunities for drinking. Threats of violence or other means of coercion may accompany all 'suggestions'. The survivor may be physically forced to take the drug. Or she may have her drink or food spiked. Chris describes:

I was being forced to take drugs – which were usually incorporated into non-consensual S/M scenes. I was always too weak or too stoned to

consider physical defence, and I had no emotional resources to draw on. The drugs I was being given also made me unable to grasp reality.

The response of the alcohol- and drug-abuse support services to the needs of lesbians and their partners has not been positive. We could not even persuade any of the known agencies to give us an interview. Most simply did not reply. There are, however, a few organisations which provide support for women who are substance users, and some are open to the establishment of lesbian and gay groups (see 'Information and resources'). Delilah relates her misgivings:

There were no services that I could go to for help. What I did look at was a women's alcohol project – they had a drop-in for women in abusive relationships, and I wanted to go. But I never went in the end: it didn't seem to deal with sexuality.

It seems that many counsellors and agencies either make no effort towards including lesbian sexuality in their programmes or name the sexuality itself as the problem. This further alienates both the abuser and the survivor. As Schilit, Lie and Montagne conclude in their paper:

One of the most compelling implications is the need for a safe environment with culturally sensitive workers, which would enable both the victims and batterers to confront their issues and resolve them. Unless social services are accountable to battered lesbians, victimised women cannot be safe.

Cycle of abuse theory

She'd been physically abused as a child and she'd had a pretty rough ride. I was fucked up about my childhood too, but her stuff was so bad she couldn't hear me. She really did love me, nurtured me, held me in a way I'd never known before. But I could only accept that love if I accepted the abuse as well. Kate

Simply explained, the cycle of abuse theory predicts that those who have been abused as children will develop into abusers themselves. If the survivors are not directly implicated in acts of abuse towards others, they are considered to make subconscious decisions to choose abusive partners. It is an analysis which provides the survivor with no personal agency and, by extension, no future free from abuse.

It is a theory which is regularly used to explain the behaviour of violent men, awarding them a 'victim' status and providing them with an excuse for their abuse. But it is becoming discredited as an infallible explanation among some of those working with survivors of child abuse today. Liz Kelly explains why she believes the theory has become so popular, both within dominant culture and among those who have been abused. In 'Outrageous Injustice', she suggests:

Recognising the deliberateness of abusers' behaviour is disturbing. It is more comfortable to believe abusers or their partners are merely repeating what they learned in childhood.

The cycle of abuse theory is, in fact, gender specific: it is concerned with men and socially endorsed masculine behaviour. Women, by contrast, are more likely to turn their abusive experiences inwards, and are less likely to re-enact their abuse on others. Three times as many girl-children are abused as boys, yet male abusers outnumber female abusers by a factor of ten to one (Kelly, Regan and Burton, 'An exploratory study of the prevalence of sexual abuse in a sample of 1200 16-21-year-olds'). The statistics disprove the validity of the theory in predicting the future behaviour of abused girl-children.

Although we should not dismiss the role of childhood abuse in adult violence, it is important to remember that a traumatic childhood does not necessarily create a destructive or self-destructive adult. Childhood abuse may in certain cases provide us with a partial explanation for an adult's desire to abuse, but it does not operate as a justification. We all make choices and decisions in our lives. We all have the *choice* to use or dismiss the use of violence in our relationships. Repeating abusive behaviour learned in the lap of the father does not relieve that original sin. Fists are not therapy.

Crimes committed against us before we can even communicate effectively will find their release in more physical expressions. It is painful and near impossible to articulate in neat sentences experiences from a time before vocabulary. Yet women do. They survive honestly, and they do not abuse their lovers. Promoting the idea that abuse inevitably begets more abuse is as dangerous for survivors as it is inaccurate and misguided. As Kelly concludes:

When we promote flawed models as 'facts' we affect social perception and understanding. Whose interest does it serve if children, adolescents and adults who have experienced sexual abuse believe that it is inevitable that they will abuse and/or that they will never be able to live ordinary/ extraordinary lives?

Internalised homophobia

Studies of the effects of racism and sexism have shown that oppressed groups often internalise their oppression. They come to believe in and feel responsible for myths perpetrated about them, distortions designed to justify their unequal treatment and victimisation by wider society. We are all affected by mainstream perceptions of 'the lesbian', and if we do not confront the stereotypes we may internalise damaging notions of what a lesbian is, leading to self-disgust, discomfort at the expression of our sexuality and guilt. If such a woman attempts to form a committed relationship, the guilt associated with her desire for sexual and social contact with other lesbians could become intensified and result in violence or self-abuse.

As Schilit, Lie and Montagne write in their paper, 'Substance Use as a Correlate of Violence in Intimate Lesbian Relationships':

Anger over societal rejection may be projected on to other lesbians, possibly resulting in abuse. Or it may be repressed, resulting in depression and feelings of powerlessness and isolation.

Power and control

There are women who use violence to coerce, to get control, to gain power; and to do that quite calculatedly in a world where they have no social power. Julie Bindel

All women are damaged by the experience of being 'woman'. We are a disempowered people, with little or no social control. Our ancestry, our story, is one of oppression. Our heritage is one of struggle. We continually search for new ways to emancipate ourselves. In spite of the territory secured for and by women over the last century, we are still living within a structure which is oppressive, in which we have little control over definitions, in which it is literally not safe to be a woman.

A woman consistently denied access to public life and social power may attempt to redress her feelings of powerlessness within her personal relationships. That this may be more possible within a lesbian relationship, where there is a clearer equality between the partners, is a sad irony. Women who use violence against other women understand it to be the most effective method of control. The abuser is empowered by the degradation and colonisation of her lover. With each punch she moves further away from the status of 'victim' herself. Cuca Hepburn elaborates:

...they have learned a lesson fundamental to a society that teaches people to victimise in order to avoid being victims. 'Alive and Well', page 170

Many abusers believe themselves to be reacting to an oppression enacted against them. They respond in self-defence. They attack their lovers in an attempt to protect themselves. They may feel threatened by their partner's class, age, race, physical ability or appearance. They may simply feel threatened by the vulnerability of loving. But we all have a choice about how we deal with our insecurities. In a paper presented to Womens Aid Federation of England, Bernie Parks explains:

...emotional and physical violence are used as effective tools of power and control and the abuser makes a choice about using that violence. We can no longer afford to view violence as a male phenomenon, but as a control issue.

Whether an abuser controls in order to gain power or not, that is the effect of her actions – although the power secured is limited to the relationship. Unlike male abusers, she will not be rewarded for her ability to control others, and she is more likely to conceal her behaviour from the wider world.

Response of the community

I'm into washing dirty laundry, because then it gets clean. Delilah

Surviving the survival process can be as painful and demoralising as undergoing the abuse itself. Certainly it leaves as many marks. The silence stifling discussion of violent lesbian relationships has been ubiquitous. Silence not only signifies the absence of debate, but also active disbelief – from close friends as well as professionals. There seems to be a common refusal to confront abuse, an embarrassment rather than a rage. Women may listen, they may even nod occasionally and buy you a drink, but at some level they seem incapable of trusting the truth of your words. There is as much fear to be found in those listening as there is in those disclosing. The sense of betrayal among survivors is profound.

Charlie was forced out of the home she shared with two friends when one of them became involved with an abusive lover. The lover threatened her way into becoming a part of the household, finally physically attacking Charlie. Both she and her flatmate moved out and attempted to warn and seek support from their local community:

When I was beaten I was bruised everywhere. Lots of women saw my bruises, including a Doc Marten print on my breast. When Julie [the abused partner] finally spoke out publicly about her beatings and feelings of disempowerment, women listened – and then rejected everything we had said. Lots of women opened their doors to Fay [the abusive partner] and made her welcome in their homes. When I confronted one of them, she said, 'I need to make my own decisions about Fay.' I felt betrayed. What did this woman need to do to make other women on the lesbian scene say, 'No: we will not allow you to treat women so badly'? Did she have to kill one of us?

The prevalent policy of non-intervention even extends to withholding information about women known to be violent from their present partners. Women are allowed to walk into injury for the sake of 'not wanting to interfere'. Kate didn't discover that her lover had a reputation for violence until after the relationship had ended:

She used to fight other people; she was really violent. She had been to

court for Actual Bodily Harm, and was known on the scene for violence.

Other women talked about their fear of hurting their abusive lovers if they revealed their behaviour to friends or outside agencies. As women, we are trained to protect and, even worse, to *understand* our abusive partners. This further secures our silence. Sarah describes:

...mostly I didn't seek support – I felt as though it would be an even further betrayal of her if I let people know how much she was really 'off her head'.

The absence of safe spaces for abused lesbians and the lack of discussion of the issue make it difficult to speak out. We may not want to be seen as 'different', may be afraid of being accused of complicity in the abuse or of being unable to cope. The fewer women who speak out, the more survivors' stories will be doubted, or their experience put down to the fact that they are somehow defective lesbians who haven't made the grade. Silence is a condoner of violence.

There are a number of reasons given for the lesbian communities' denial of lesbian violence. The most obvious is that as a community under attack, we need to protect ourselves from outside criticism. We need to concentrate on fighting homophobia, sexism and racism; admitting to flaws or divisions is a dangerous distraction and releases information that can be appropriated by the heterosexual enemy in attempts to discredit us further. As Avedon Carol of Feminists against Censorship suggests:

It's the dirty secret. Lesbians are a family, and like all families we don't want other people to know what goes on behind closed doors.

Liz Kelly in 'Unspeakable Acts' writes of the reasons for the silence and its long-term effects on the survivor:

Voicing this publicly seems to undercut not only our political analysis of male power and heterosexuality, but also our optimism about lesbian relationships. This collective refusal has been, in part, responsible for the difficulty many lesbians have in naming their experience as abuse or violence, especially if it includes coercive sex.

The 'optimism' Kelly refers to is also known as the 'lesbian utopia': an idealised and sanitised vision of lesbian relationships and lifestyles. In our scramble to create alternatives to the pathological models popular in wider society and the media, we have opted to present the polar opposite as a truer representation.

We don't want to be seen as imperfect. Everyone thinks that it is wrong to be a lesbian anyway, so there is a tremendous pressure to give an image of stable relationships. Femi Otitoju

We have had to fight hard to create this image of a homogenous caring and compassionate lesbian community, for the idea of the dyke scene as a superior zone. The lesbian utopia has also arisen from a feminist rejection of heterosexuality, of male oppression and values and a perception of ourselves as 'not men' and as not emotionally contracted to men. If male dominance means oppression, then life without men means freedom and equality. But in order to move towards a community that is truly more compassionate and has more integrity, we must learn to accept a more accurate picture of ourselves. Only then may we improve upon it.

A protection of the lesbian community by denying that violence happens and by minimising either its effect or its prevalence is counter-productive. It's not useful and it's not necessary. We should be able to develop a feminist analysis around violence, but it has got to be a feminist one. Julie Bindel

Services

Seeking out services that deal intelligently and compassionately with lesbian abuse was a long and frustrating process. Many of the women's organisations we contacted did not reply, or were unable to offer us help in our research, citing only the vaguest of reasons for their effective non-cooperation. The typical response was guarded. And so it seems that although lesbians have been instrumental in the formation of services for abused heterosexual women, a similar network is not yet in existence for dykes themselves.

If we look at the American example, we can see both how far we need to travel and how far it is possible to go. During the 1980s the National Coalition Against Domestic Violence Lesbian Task Force organised the Lesbian Abuse Issues Network to explore lesbian violence and abuse in detail for the first time. Their early research provided the basis for an initial political analysis and led to a series of recommendations for the practical support of survivors. Thirteen years ago Woman Inc. was established as the only non-residential service institute for abused women in the US. Based in California, the centre has developed a comprehensive programme for tackling the issue of abuse and providing support for survivors, including individual and group therapy for both abused partners and women who want to overcome their violent behaviour. The centre also provides a twenty-four-hour crisis line, legal advice and information and can refer women on to appropriate agencies. Consultation and training are also available for shelters, lesbian and gay organisations, medical and mental-health services, advocates and universities.

In Britain, the Womens Aid Federation of England (WAFE), which is responsible for 270 separate refuges throughout the country, is beginning tentatively to address lesbian domestic violence. WAFE runs training workshops on service provisions for lesbians. But as Caroline McKinlay of WAFE explains:

The degree to which refuge groups actively promote their services to their local lesbian community depends largely upon their resources and awareness of the issue. At a national level, the profile of lesbians within the organisation is ensured through workshops at our conference and the National Lesbians in Womens Aid group.

In other words, although the issue is beginning to be considered seriously at a national level, training and practical assistance have not yet filtered down to all refuges. In fact, some refuge workers have expressed open discomfort at the idea of accepting abused lesbians into their safe houses: they fear that limited resources may be withdrawn by homophobic local authorities and are unsure about what support they can give a lesbian survivor. Psychologist Nancy Hammond describes the problems encountered in the American experience in her paper 'Lesbian Victims of Relationship Violence':

Many funders or other community members have only reluctantly come to accept the idea that heterosexual battering reflects male oppression of women. When shelter workers or advocates meet a situation that appears to defy their own understanding and analysis, the battered lesbian herself is seen as the problem.

Fear of homophobia within refuges acts as a further deterrent to lesbians seeking sanctuary. Refuges remain a heterosexual environment, tuned to the needs of heterosexual women escaping violence from men. Vicky Watson, a refuge worker within a Women's Aid Ltd shelter (one of one-third of refuges not affiliated to WAFE) describes the extent of the problem and attitudes to it:

Homophobia is rife in refuges. Women's Aid doesn't address it at all, and that really infuriates me. You can go to lesbian support groups, but they are mainly for affiliated refuges. It has something to do with the fact that domestic violence and refuges are seen as heterosexual issues. There is not enough written down on paper, and there is not enough effective training around this issue.

Homophobia within refuges has led to suggestions that a lesbian-only shelter, independently organised and funded, should be established. This would certainly ensure a non-heterosexist environment, and would mean that the issue would be focused on fully rather than in a tokenistic way. There could be other, less welcome consequences from a lesbian-only refuge, however. Vicky Watson is cautious:

My main concern when I heard that there may be a solitary lesbian refuge was that because the dyke community is relatively small, it wouldn't take too long before that refuge was pretty well known within the community. And then how safe are the women going to be?

A lesbian-only refuge is also unlikely to be awarded funding, so perhaps a more realistic solution lies in adapting the services of the refuges already in existence.

I'm not saying that there isn't a need for refuges for lesbians, but at the same time that shouldn't be a reason for not making the refuges that already exist more able to support lesbians. Creating a refuge for lesbians doesn't alter the fact that there will still be issues that will have to be dealt with around race, around class and around other power differentials. Liz Kelly

The purpose of a refuge is to provide temporary secure accommodation while helping the survivor to find a more permanent living space. In order for a local authority to extend its help to re-housing the battered woman, she must fulfil requirements specified in Part III of the Housing Act (1985). Some refuges cite the Housing Act as a reason for preferring not to give space to lesbians (although none is actively turned away). The Act specifies that a woman must be classified as both 'homeless' and in 'priority need' in order to qualify for assistance. To count as priority need, a woman must either be pregnant or have children or be classified as belonging to a vulnerable group: under-16s, or women with alcohol or drug problems, mental-health difficulties, or special needs. Some lesbians may meet these requirements, but they are less likely to be fleeing with children than their heterosexual counterparts. In addition, local authorities increasingly demand official evidence of priority need: statements from the police, doctors or social services. Since few lesbians report domestic violence, such evidence is difficult to collate. If the survivor does contact an agency for help, it is likely to be a voluntary women's organisation whose testimony is often afforded little credibility.

Lesbian and Gay Switchboard provides no core training for operators in dealing with women who have been beaten or sexually assaulted by other women, though guest speakers are invited to discuss specific concerns. Callers are often advised to contact Women's Aid or Rape Crisis Line. There are two self-help groups for lesbians living in London, though both are now over-subscribed. Pain and Strength was formed in 1992, and the West Hampstead Women's Centre organised a group in early 1993. Both work towards providing information about violence between women and offer a supportive environment in which women may disclose their stories.

It is obvious that further provisions for the lesbian survivor must be made within the existing support organisations. It is also obvious that it will take time, money and human resources to fulfil our needs.

The future

I feel that it is individuals who create abuse in any community, but acknowledging its existence is a starting point. I feel that lesbians are too good at quoting myths of 'sisterhood' rather than being there for each other in a non-judgemental, compassionate way. Chris

Clearly many changes need to be made within our communities and outside in order for the issues raised within this book to be adequately addressed. We need to develop our services so that special provision is made for dykes fleeing abuse, we need to alter our attitude to both the abused and the abuser, we need to feel safe enough to evolve a public analysis, we need to uncover and reject the myths that prevent us from confronting the problem. We need to slice through the silence.

It begins with belief. No progress is possible unless and until the abused woman feels safe enough to disclose her story.

I think it is really important that the lesbian community takes it on. So that if a lesbian needs help and turns to her friends they aren't going to say that nothing happened. That it is believed is what is really important; and that's where I think it has to develop. Jean Cross

I believe that we should stop protecting women who do not control their violence or are abusive to other women in any way. It is still secret: hush, hush. Admitting it exists is one step forward. Jo

Breaking the silence is a priority, but equally important is how that silence is broken. Many of the women we interviewed emphasised the need for open debate, and for more information and training to be provided.

I want there to be forums for women to be able to talk about it. I would have got so much from that. I want space for women to talk, and support. We need to look at mental abuse – we can't ignore that mental abuse can be so powerful. Delilah

Alongside debate comes the acceptance of diversity within our communities. We need to understand the full facts, and this can only be done once we have shaken off our preconceived notions about sado-masochism, or butch-femme, or class or colour. Bigotry simply equals further silence.

It's crucial that we move away from this neurotic need for us all to be the same. We are not all middle class, we don't all have nice comfortable homes, we don't all come from situations where we can resolve our problems because we can afford to visit a therapist two or three times a week. And we need to develop a vocabulary for dealing with this. We should open up, allow diversity. Anna

In the US, women's organisations have set up therapy programmes which work with both the survivor and the abuser. How far are we prepared to work with female abusers? Some would argue for the absolute exclusion of abusive partners, not only from therapy programmes but from the lesbian social circuit. Some survivors are tired of protecting abusers from themselves and from exposure.

If women continue to accept women abusers into our community, how can we ever protect ourselves and demand change from those who seek to hurt us? Charlie

But there is a huge difference between protecting by silence and working actively with the abuser to control her violence and understand its roots.

I don't think that to exclude women who are being violent from every social context, and from places where she may eventually get support and help in stopping, is acceptable. Why isolate her? I think we should isolate men: they have the whole world. But it is not the same for lesbians: if you exclude her from one social situation, she will just move on to another, and she won't have got her act together. She will go and be violent in another situation. We need to look seriously at what help and support we can provide for women who are violent, alongside providing support for women who face that violence. Julie Bindel

We need to find ways in which more support groups can be formed and funded. We need to ensure that the advice given survivors is useful, and that their perception of the lesbian scene is not further damaged by the response their disclosures receive. Much of the work undertaken will be at the expense of those women who volunteer their time, energy and skills. And any changes must be on a nationwide level: it is not sufficient to have support groups in London when there is a woman bleeding in Newcastle. A possible first step would be the installation of a national helpline, which would concern itself with advice to lesbians and gay men who find themselves in abusive situations. In the meantime, we must improve upon established services, and work towards securing the resources for new initiatives.

What we need is some kind of 'drop in' where we have women who feel ready and able to deal with whatever comes up in that context, so that there is the possibility of a more immediate support. But in a context where even running a group feels like stretching beyond the resources that some women have, I'm aware that it's asking an awful lot. Liz Kelly

Information and resources

Emergency numbers

London Rape Crisis Tel: 071 837 1600. 24-hour service. Can refer callers to non-London services and to local refuges.

Women's Aid Tel: 0272 633 542. 24-hour service. Has contacts for Asian, African-Caribbean, Chinese and South American women. Also gives legal advice.

Lesbian survivors' groups

Pain and Strength c/o London Women's Centre, Wesley House, 4 Wild Court, London WC2B 4AU. Self-help group, write for introduction.

Survivors of Abusive Lesbian Relationships c/o West Hampstead Women's Centre, 55 Hemstal Road, London NW6. Tel: 071 328 7389. Self-help support for lesbians who have experienced emotional, physical or sexual abuse in a lesbian relationship. Phone for details.

Counselling and support

Black Lesbian and Gay Centre Arch 196, Bellenden Road, London SE14. Tel: 071 732 3885. Counselling and advice.

Camden Lesbian Centre/Black Lesbian Group 54-56 Phoenix Road, London NW1. Tel: 071 383 5405. Counselling and housing advice.

Gemma Box BM 5700, London WC1 3XX. Group for disabled lesbians.

London Friend 86 Caledonian Road, London N1 9DN. Tel: 071 837 2782. Counselling helpline and support groups for lesbians and gay men. Specific groups for black lesbians. Induction loop, ramp, adapted toilet and lift.

North London Line Tel: 071 607 8346. Aims to empower young lesbians via assertiveness training, discussions on relationships, etc. Provides short-term counselling. All staff are lesbian and gay. For lesbians under 25.

PACE 34 Hartman Road, London N7 9JL. Tel: 071 700 1323. Advice and information for lesbians and gay men. Offers crisis intervention and ongoing counselling.

Positively Women 5 Sebastian Street, London N1. Tel: 071 490 2327. Advice, information and support for all women affected by HIV/AIDS.

Survivors of Abuse Tel: 071 482 6371. Therapy group for women survivors and their partners.

Teenage Information Network 102 Harper Road, London SE1 6AQ. Tel: 071 403 2444. Advice, information and counselling. Has African-Caribbean counsellor. General information on benefits and housing.

Women's Therapy Centre 6-9 Manor Gardens, London N7 6LA. Tel: 071 263 6200. Offers individual and group therapy. Prioritises lesbian users. Sliding fee scale.

Helplines

Black Lesbian and Gay Centre Tel: 081 732 3885. Tues and Thurs 2-4.30pm.

Jewish Lesbian and Gay Helpline Tel: 071 706 3123. Mon and Thurs 7-10pm.

Lesbian and Gay Switchboard Tel: 071 837 7324. Can put you in touch with local switchboards and helplines. 24-hour service.

London Friend Women's Line Tel: 071 837 2782. Tues and Thurs 7.30-10pm.

London Lesbian Line Tel: 071 251 6911. Mon and Fri 2-10pm. Tues, Wed and Thurs 7-10pm.

Substance abuse

Angel Drug Project Tel: 071 226 3113. Counselling for drug users. Has lesbian members of staff.

Drink Crisis Centre Women's Services Tel: 071 252 6900.

SCODA Tel: 071 928 9500. National directory of services for drug users.

Women's Alcohol Centre 66A Drayton Park, London N5 1ND. Tel: 071 226 4581. Confidential counselling, groups and workshops for lesbians with alcohol problems.

Housing

Council housing information can be obtained from local District Housing Offices, which include Homeless Persons Units.

Stonewall Housing Association Tel: 071 359 5767. Advice on lesbian and gay housing rights.

Health

Audre Lorde Clinic Tel: 071 377 7312. **Bernhard Clinic** Tel: 081 846 1577. Lesbian sexual health clinics offering comprehensive advice on sexual health as well as counselling.

Women's Health 52-54 Featherstone Street, London EC1Y 8RT. Tel: 071 251 6580. Information and resource library.

Legal

GLAD (Gay Legal Advice) Tel: 071 253 2043, Mon-Fri 7-10pm. Free and confidential legal advice over the phone.

Joint Council for the Welfare of Immigrants 115 Old Street, London EC1Y 8RT. Tel: 071 251 8706.

Lesbian Custody Project c/o Rights of Women, 52-54 Featherstone Street, London EC1Y 8RT. Tel: 071 251 6575/6/7.

Rights of Women As above. Legal advice and support.

For advice on benefits contact **DSS Freeline Social Security** Tel: 0800 666555. Most towns have a **Law Centre** or **Citizens Advice Bureau**.

Legal options

The police service and the judicial system are known for their sexism, racism and homophobia. As lesbians, a lot of us have little faith in their ability to protect us. Added to this is the unwritten lesbian law that women do not report other women to the police. This would be acceptable if we had mechanisms to cope with abusive women. But we don't. A lesbian may suffer a lot more than a heterosexual woman before going to the police and her abuser may exploit her reluctance. It is important that women understand that it is their right to be protected.

What follows is an outline of the available options; in addition, advice can be sought from Law Centres and Citizens Advice Bureaus or from Women's Aid (Tel: 0272 633 542) who will sometimes accompany women to the police, solicitor or court.

The police

This is the only agency with powers of intervention available on a 24-hour basis. A few stations have Domestic Violence Units, staffed by plain-clothes officers, though the response given an abused lesbian will depend on the training and attitude of individual members of staff. The units should explain the range of actions available to you and can be contacted for advice outside times of crisis.

The police can be asked to:
- respond quickly to a call
- listen to the survivor independently of her abuser
- keep records of all incidents of violence
- accompany you back home and stand by to prevent a breach of the peace while you collect essential belongings
- arrange transport to a refuge

The police will also try to:
- arrest the abuser where there is sufficient evidence to arrest for a criminal offence, breach of bail conditions or of an injunction
- arrange for immediate medical aid

The police can arrest the abuser for:
Common Assault Threats of violence or hitting without causing an injury
Assault Occasioning Actual Bodily Harm (ABH) Violence that results in injury – whether a visible physical injury or pain and soreness
Grievous Bodily Harm (GBH) Violence that causes serious injury or was intended to cause serious injury

Malicious Wounding An assault with or without a weapon in which the skin is broken

If the abused partner wants her abuser warned but not arrested, the police can issue a formal **Caution**. This can be useful if the violence continues and the abused partner wants her abuser arrested at a later date.

If the abuser is arrested and charged with an offence, she may be released on bail. **Bail conditions**, which are set by the court, usually state that the abuser is to keep away from the injured party. You can ask the police to inform you of:

- when the abuser has been released, whether on bail or otherwise
- whether the abuser has been charged
- any action taken, including forthcoming court appearances

Solicitors

Regional or national helplines may be able to put you in touch with solicitors known to be sympathetic.

Injunctions

These are court orders that instruct the abuser to do or not to do certain things. They can be secured via a solicitor or directly from the court. If the terms of an injunction are broken, police can arrest. Police may suggest you take out an injunction rather than arresting the abuser, though you can ask for an arrest if you think it appropriate.

Going to court

The police recommend prosecution to the Crown Prosecution Service if they deem it appropriate. The CPS then decides whether or not to go ahead and, depending on the charge, whether the case should be heard before magistrates or in the Crown Court. There may be a commital hearing in the Crown Court to decide if there is enough evidence to proceed. Always try to find someone to accompany you to court and ask the Clerk of the Court to keep your address confidential. If her assailant is found guilty, the survivor can apply for a compensation order as part of the sentence.

Preparing evidence

It is essential that all details of the abuses enacted against you be recorded in order to present a strong case for prosecution or protection. The following is a checklist of proof required for women who are considering legal action:

- Keep a **log book** of all abusive incidents. Included in this should be the **date and time** the incident took place, a **description of the**

abuse, and full details of any **action taken.**
- Take **photographs of any injuries, to the self or to property.** Try to get the photographs **witnessed** by a responsible adult.
- **Report** any incidents of harassment or violence **to the police.**
- Have any **injuries** sustained **examined** by a doctor.
- Gather statements from any **witnesses to the violence.**
- With reference to **property disputes: keep receipts of repair bills, proof of separate rent payments, details of purchase of specific items.** It is also advisable to have your name on any tenancy contract.

All of the above are not only useful in proceeding with civil action, but may in themselves be used to confront the abuser. It may be enough to persuade her to cease intimidation and harassment.

A lesbian is entitled to the same rights as any citizen. In an emergency she should have every confidence that her 999 call will be responded to without prejudice. Her support network should back her up if she decides on this route for her protection. She should not have to suffer alone.

Further reading

Bell, Ellen, 'With our own Hands', *Trouble and Strife* 16, Summer 1989.

Califia, Pat, 'A House Divided: Violence in the Lesbian S/M Community', *Bratt Attack* 1.

Clunis, Merilee D., Green, Dorsey G., *Lesbian Couples*, Seal Press, 1988.

Davis, Maggie, 'Gays may get protection from violent partners', *Pink Paper*, May 1992.

Hall, Alison, 'Abuse in Lesbian Relationships', *Trouble and Strife* 23, Spring 1992.

Hammond, Nancy, 'Lesbian Victims of Relationship Violence', *Journal of Homosexuality*, Haworth Press, 1989.

Hepburn, Cuca, *Alive and Well: Lesbian Health Guide*, Crossing Press, 1988.

Kelly, Liz, 'Outrageous Injustice', *Community Care*, June 1992.

Kelly, Liz, 'Unspeakable Acts', *Trouble and Strife* 21, Summer 1991.

Lobel, Kerry, ed., *Naming the Violence; Speaking out about Lesbian Battering*, Seal Press, 1986.

London Borough of Camden, 'Domestic Violence' information and advice pack, available free. Tel: 071 860 5947.

NiCarthy, Ginny, *Getting Free: A Handbook for Women in Abusive Situations*, Journeyman Press, 1982.

Renzetti, Clair, *Violent Betrayal*, Sage, 1992.

Schilit, Lie and Montagne, 'Substance Use as a Correlate of Violence in Intimate Lesbian Relationships', *Journal of Homosexuality*, Haworth Press, 1990.